The Normans and their Myth

R. H. C. DAVIS

The Normans
and their Myth

with 69 illustrations,
12 in colour

THAMES AND HUDSON

LONDON

Frontispiece: Durham Cathedral. Vaults of north
nave aisle, *c.* 1100–28.

© 1976 THAMES AND HUDSON LTD, LONDON

Printed and bound in Great Britain by
Jarrold and Sons Ltd, Norwich

Contents

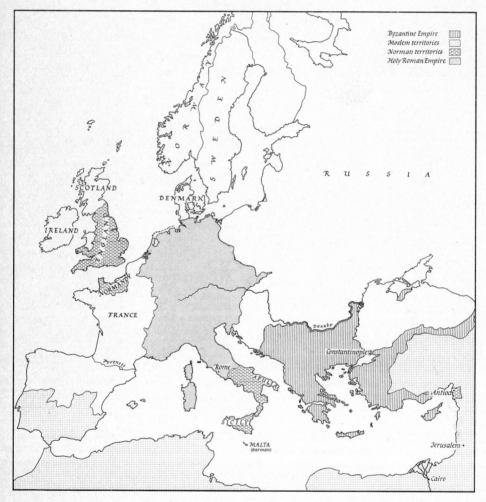

2 The Norman conquests.

Introduction

The Normans are renowned both for their conquests and for the way in which they adopted, and often improved upon, the civilization of the peoples they conquered. Descended from the Scandinavian Northmen who were granted the duchy in 911, the Normans had hastened to acquire the civilization of the Franks and had succeeded in doing so without losing their martial virtue. By the second half of the eleventh century they were in the front rank of European civilization, famous for their monasteries, their schools and their architecture, but still unsurpassed in war.

The most famous of their conquests was that of England in 1066. It was quick, complete and permanent, and as a result of it the Normans became some of the richest people in Europe, and their Duke was made a king. But at much the same time individual knights from Normandy were making conquests in Italy and Sicily. They acquired Aversa in 1030, Apulia and Calabria in 1059 and most of Sicily by 1072. In addition they launched expeditions against the Byzantine Empire on the mainland of Greece (1082–4), and under the leadership of Bohemond ('the giant') played a prominent part in the First Crusade and acquired the principality of Antioch (1098).

The Normans themselves liked to attribute these conquests to their innate martial valour, but most historians have been more impressed by the excellence of their military institutions. Though not the first people to make use of feudalism – the system of raising an army by dividing the land into knights' fiefs – they exploited it to the full

7

while keeping it strictly in control; in England they compiled Domesday Book (1086) as an exhaustive inventory of the king's lands, and in Italy the *Catalogus Baronum* (*c.* 1175) as a catalogue of fiefs. Similarly, though they were by no means the first people to build castles, the Normans were quick to appreciate their value, and built them in enormous numbers, in order to ensure the continued subjection of the peoples they had conquered.

The Normans did not allow their warlike activities to submerge the arts of civilization. In Normandy the school of the abbey of Bec was under the control of the two most famous intellects of the age, Lanfranc (*c.* 1044–66) and Anselm (1066–93), and attracted pupils from all parts of Europe. After the conquest of England, Lanfranc and Anselm were successive archbishops of Canterbury (1070–89 and 1093–1109 respectively) and reformed the English Church so successfully that monks of theirs were invited to found new monasteries, or become bishops, in Scotland, Wales and Ireland. Norman architecture also had a high reputation. The cathedrals and abbeys built in England were among the largest and most splendid in Western Europe, and excited the admiration of all who saw them. King David I adopted the style for his new abbeys in Scotland – the nave of Dunfermline (1128–50) being a frank imitation of Durham – while further afield at the cathedral of St Magnus at Kirkwall in Orkney (begun 1138) or Cormac's chapel at Cashel in central Ireland (*c.* 1134) the influence of the Normans was equally apparent.

As if this was not enough, the Normans of Italy and Sicily fostered a different civilization which, with its strange mixture of Latin, Greek and Arabic elements, acted as a sort of intellectual clearing-house between East and West. Scholars travelled all the way from Northern Europe to find books on Greek philosophy, Greek mathematics or Greek science at the court of King Roger II who, in the course of his patronage of the arts, supported, among others, the Arab geographer al-Edrisi for fifteen years at his court (1139–54). The brilliant civilization which resulted can easily be appreciated in monuments such as the cathedrals of Cefalù (1131–48) and Monreale (1172–89) or the Capella Palatina at Palermo (1132–70). With their Byzantine mosaics, honeycomb ceilings, pointed arches and occasional inscriptions in Greek or Arabic, they seem to form a world apart from England and Normandy; and because of them many scholars have suggested that the Normans were among the most adaptable, tolerant and understanding patrons of culture that history has known.

The most puzzling feature of the Normans is the way they disappeared. England had an Angevin king from 1154, Sicily a German from 1194, and in 1204 Normandy was lost to the French. Though the heirs of Bohemond ruled over the last remnants of the principality of Antioch till 1287, they no longer thought of themselves as Normans. The people who had dominated so many aspects of Europe in the eleventh and twelfth centuries, in the thirteenth century had simply disappeared. How can this be explained?

9

3 Coin of Richard I of Normandy (942–96).

4 Coin of Roger I, Great Count of Sicily (d. 1101).

5, 6 More Norman than the Normans. *Opposite:* St Magnus's Cathedral at
Kirkwall, begun in 1137, seems wholly Norman, although the Orkneys
were not under Norman rule. By contrast, the Capella Palatina in Palermo
(*above*), which was built for the Norman kings of Sicily (1132–70), seems
Byzantine or Arabic.

The more one studies the history of the Normans, the more one is bound to question who or what they were. It is almost impossible to pin them down because they kept on changing. In the first place they were Northmen, that is to say Scandinavian pirates, and pagan. In the year 911, or thereabouts, King Charles the Simple ceded to them the territory between the Epte and the sea, and as a result that land became known as the land of the Northmen, *Northmannia*, which was soon to be shortened to *Normannia* or Normandy. A century later the Normans no longer looked or sounded like Northmen; they had given up piracy and become Christian, and were no longer speaking a Scandinavian language, but French. Indeed other people often thought they *were* French.

In 1066 the Anglo-Saxon Chronicle described two famous battles. In the first, which was the Battle of Stamford Bridge, it said that the English King Harold defeated the *Normen*. In the second, which was at Hastings, it said that the same King Harold was defeated by the French (*frencyscan*). This was no slip of the pen. The Chronicle always called the Normans 'Frenchmen'; Edward the Confessor's favourites were not Norman but 'French', the great barons of William I and William II were 'French', and even in 1127 it was all the 'French' and English who were offended when Henry I married his daughter to an Angevin. Similarly in their charters the Norman kings, though they styled themselves 'king of the English and duke of the Normans', always addressed their subjects as 'French and English'. It was as if the definition of a Norman at this date was a Frenchman from Normandy.

It is not very difficult to guess why this change occurred. In many parts of North-West Europe, particularly in Germany, the term *Nordmanni* still referred (as in Adam of Bremen) to the Danes or Norwegians, and *Nordmannia* to Norway. Once the Normans of Normandy had abandoned paganism and piracy and learnt to speak a civilized language, it was natural that they, and everyone else, would want to distinguish them from the sort of Northmen who were still little better than northern pirates. In the same way the descendants of the Normans who had settled in England were generally called English by the end of the twelfth century, in order to distinguish them from their enemies the French.

In some cases it is extremely difficult to decide who was, and who was not, a Norman. The last member of the royal house of Norman Sicily is said to have been Constance, but she married the Emperor Henry VI and gave birth, in 1194, to the child who was to become the Emperor Frederick II; by historical convention he is called a German, but one wonders whether he would not have been called a Norman if he had not become Emperor but remained King of Sicily. On the other hand a modern historical convention gives us 'Normans' in twelfth-century Ireland and Scotland, though hardly anyone would have described them as such at the time – in Ireland they were 'English' and in Scotland 'French'.[1] One cannot help wondering what the definition of a Norman should be. Must he have lived or been born in Normandy, or would it be sufficient if he came of a family with a Norman name? And if the latter, how remote could his ancestry be? Would it have been enough if one of his great-grandparents had been a Norman?

In spite of these difficulties, historians have been convinced that the Normans were a separate and distinct people. Charles Homer Haskins, Evelyn Jamison and David Douglas – to name only the most distinguished of this century – have argued vigorously for the common identity of the Normans, whether they lived in Normandy, England, Sicily or Antioch. They have written of 'the

[1] For references, see pp. 134 et seq.

Norman world' and 'the unity of the Norman achievement', attempting to explain the various transformations of the Normans as being due to their 'ability to respect the traditions, and to utilize the aptitudes of those they governed'.[2] As Haskins put it:

They did their work pre-eminently not as a people apart, but as a group of leaders and energizers, the little leaven that leaveneth the whole lump. Wherever they went, they showed a marvellous power of initiative and assimilation; if the initiative is more evident in England, the assimilation is more manifest in Sicily. The penalty for such activity is rapid loss of identity; the reward is a large share in the general history of civilization. If the Normans paid the penalty, they also reaped the reward, and they were never more Norman than in adopting the statesmanlike policy of toleration and assimilation which led to their ultimate extinction.[3]

The question which this passage prompts is how often a people can transform itself and yet remain the same. The development suggested is that the Normans were first Scandinavian Northmen and then transformed themselves by a 'statesmanlike policy' first into Norman-French and subsequently into Anglo-Norman, Sicilian-Norman and the rest. But if we ask why these last names are more suitable than 'Anglo-French' or 'Sicilian-French', the answer must be that that was how the Normans wrote their history. It is their conviction which has convinced us.

The Norman historian of the twelfth century who was most eloquent about the unity and Normanness of the Normans was Orderic Vitalis. He was a monk of Saint-Evroul in Normandy, and wrote of the Normans in Apulia and Normandy as if they formed one great family with constant comings and goings between them. The unity of the Norman achievement was 'all real to him, and through him to us', wrote Miss Jamison, 'because it was accomplished by his friends from the valley of the Risle.'[4]

That is undeniable. But how many other Normans had such friends? In Chapters 2 and 3 we will give reasons for thinking that Orderic, though he was writing from his own experience, was in a position which was rare, if not unique, in Normandy, and which does not seem to have been shared by anyone in Italy.

Nonetheless, by writing in the way he did, Orderic has persuaded almost all subsequent historians of the reality of the Norman world. As Dr Chibnall has written in her edition of his history:

His work laid the foundations of the epic of the Normans, not only in Normandy and England, but from Scotland to Apulia, through the Balkans to Constantinople and the Holy Land, which, in some ways, was to influence all subsequent historians of them, from Wace and Benoît of Sainte-Maure in the twelfth century to C.H. Haskins and D.C. Douglas eight hundred years later.[5]

It is a frightening thought that one eloquent historian might impose an idiosyncratic view on all his successors, compelling them to consider that disparate conditions and disjointed events were really part of an 'inherent unity';[6] and it is obviously essential to compare his work with that of his predecessors, in order to discover how far, and in what ways, he had transformed the Normans' own view of themselves.

The fact which must strike any student of the Normans is the large number of historians they produced in the eleventh and twelfth centuries; one gets the impression that they could never have stopped talking or writing about themselves. That, perhaps, is why they were so sure of their identity. For if peoples are formed, not by race or language, but by a common political, military or emotional experience, they can remain peoples only so long as that experience is kept alive, by handing on the story of it from generation to generation. Alternatively, if a nation without a history is a contradiction in terms, can it be that the only way to make a nation is by the creation of a myth?

The creation of a myth does not mean the invention of a sort of fairy story, but rather the acceptance of a belief about the past, whether that belief be false or true; and as anthropologists and sociologists have shown, a people's beliefs about the past can be used as a guide to its hopes and aspirations in the future. Examples from recent history are Hitler's belief in the Aryan race and Mussolini's belief in Italy as heir of the Roman Empire, both of which could be regarded either as a myth or as a political programme.

Most historical myths are less obvious and less blatant than these. In medieval history we cannot escape them. We have books on 'medieval Germany' and 'medieval Italy', although we know that in a general sense neither country existed as a separate entity in the Middle Ages. We do not think it unusual to have histories of 'medieval Belgium' or 'Roman Switzerland', and in this book it will prove impossible not to refer to 'France' and the 'French', since although these terms are anachronistic, the alternatives available could be even more confusing. Nonetheless, no historian can escape the fact that once a history has been written about a people, that people becomes a historical 'fact', which may in turn have a great influence on political reality; terms such as 'the history of Ireland' or 'the history of Ulster' can help to make history as well as record it.

For these reasons it seems important to discuss the Normans in the light of their myth in order to discover how they became Normans, how they changed their ideas of what a Norman was, and how eventually they lost their identity. Some of the evidence will be literary, and some drawn from art and architecture, but always we will try to keep a balance between what the Normans were and what they thought they were. We will start with two

7 The beginning of Book III of Orderic Vitalis's *Ecclesiastical History*, written in his own hand. As one of his sources he cites Dudo.

chapters on Normandy, one dealing with the reality as it is now seen by scientific history, and the other with the myth as it developed in Normandy in the eleventh and twelfth centuries. In the following chapters on Italy-Sicily and England we will discuss reality and myth together, using each to throw light on the other, in the hope that in the end we will be able to form an opinion as to whether the Normanness of the Normans was an objective reality, or merely a myth which remained effective only so long as people believed in it.

Chapter One

Normandy and the Northmen

Normandy sits astride the Lower Seine, and the Seine is a highway leading into the heart of France. It was inevitable that the Viking or Northman pirates of the ninth century would be attracted by this river, because its tributaries provided a network of waterways which covered most of northern, eastern and central France, and was ideal for their tactics. Their most lengthy expeditions up the Seine were in 856–61 and 885–91. For most of the intervening period and in 892–6 they were across the Channel making a major effort to conquer England. After they had been thwarted there they returned to the Seine. In 911, if we are to accept the traditional date, Charles the Simple, King of the Franks, ceded a large territory on the Lower Seine to a Northman called Rollo, and that cession is regarded as the foundation of Normandy. Presumably the intention was that Rollo should defend the Seine against all other invaders, but the history of Normandy is almost a complete blank for the rest of the century. Information about almost any part of France is scanty in the tenth century, but the few chroniclers there were either knew nothing about Normandy or thought it unworthy of record.

As a result there has been much imaginative speculation. Romantic historians used to suggest that the Northmen had so devastated the land that it was 'untilled by the plough, stripped of all beasts and cattle and rendered useless to men',[1] and that it had to be repopulated with Northmen who came either direct from Scandinavia, or alternatively from the Danish settlements in England and

8 The nave of the great abbey church of Jumièges, dedicated in 1067, and one of the few large churches to have survived from the period before the conquest of England.

19

Ireland. This suggestion is still popular with British tourists who are told that the effect of the Danish settlement may be seen, not only in the place-names of Normandy, but also in 'the fair-haired type of population which has persisted in many regions to this day',[2] and though those who use their eyes have invariably been disappointed, the legend dies hard. It is best, therefore, to discuss the problem.

In the first place it must be stated with all the force possible that no serious historian could accept the view that the Northmen had reduced the province to a desert. In all the ravages of war, at any rate till the advent of chemical warfare, one of the most consistent and remarkable features has been how quickly the land has recovered. The peasants never have been exterminated, the land always has been tilled at the first opportunity, and although all the villages and houses may have been destroyed, the crops reappear. There is no evidence whatsoever to suggest that things were different in the eighth or ninth century. The Northmen might have dispossessed Frenchmen and taken over their lands, but they could not have made the whole province a desert.

The problem, therefore, is essentially one of how the Northmen settled down in the province they had conquered, and how they treated the natives. Theoretically there are three main possibilities. First, they might have concentrated in certain towns such as Rouen and Bayeux, and dominated the province from those centres, in the same way as in England the Danes dominated the East Midlands from the Five Boroughs. Secondly, they might conceivably have dispossessed the existing cultivators of the soil and have taken their place, beating their swords into ploughshares and their spears into pruning-hooks; but in this case they would have had to be extraordinarily numerous, a whole race of agriculturists thwarted by the lack of cultivable land in Scandinavia. Or thirdly, if their numbers were more limited, they might simply have taken the place of the Frankish lords, enjoying the fruits of the land which would have been cultivated for them by native labour. In this case they would have formed a landed aristocracy comparable to that which their descendants established in England after 1066.

Of these three possibilities the one which is most difficult to prove or disprove is the first. Though we know there was a ducal palace at Rouen, we have practically no information about the Norman towns in the tenth century. All we can say is that when Dudo was writing (*c.* 1015–24) he obviously considered Rouen to be a large and thriving town and the centre of ducal government. In his stories about the minority of Duke Richard I he assumed that the townsmen would play an active and spontaneous part in defence of their duke against the Frankish king, but he specifically says that they spoke the 'Roman' rather than the Danish language. If the Scandinavian element in the population of the towns had been large, it is hard to believe that the Danish language could have been forgotten so soon.

There has been a great deal of discussion about the extent of Scandinavian settlement in the countryside, since place-names can furnish much evidence in this respect.[3] Some embody Scandinavian personal names, others have Scandinavian endings. The endings which have attracted most attention are *buth* (booth) as in Elbeuf, and *flo* as in Honfleur and Harfleur, but the most common one, which occurs about a hundred times, is *tot* (toft) as in Yvetot and Criquetot. Others which are fairly common are *haugr* (promontory) as in La Hogue, *gate* (road) as in Holgate (the hollow road), *marr* (mere) as in Roumare, and *bec* as in Caudebec (the cold stream) which has its exact parallel at Cawdbeck in the Lake District. It is a major difficulty, however, that many names which were once regarded as pre-eminently Scandinavian have been found to have parallels in non-Scandinavian parts of France, as in the case of Dieppe, which could mean 'deep' in English or Frisian as well as in Scandinavian, and Fécamp which (even if it is not to be derived from *fisci campus* or 'royal demesne') has been claimed as a Germanic rather than Scandinavian *fisk hafn* or 'fish harbour'. At least one of the Elbeufs is now thought to refer to a Germanic person called *Ellebod* rather than to a 'booth by the elder trees', and some of the 'hogues' might be derived from the Old English *hoh* (cliff or precipice) as easily as from the Old Norse *haugr*.

The same difficulty is to be found in distinguishing between Scandinavian and Germanic personal names. The Franks (who were Germanic) had ruled the country for more than four centuries before the settlement of the Northmen, and there was also a strong settlement of Saxons in the district round Bayeux. Though some names such as Cnut or Haakon are distinctively Scandinavian, a large number are common to the Germanic peoples generally – they include Asi, Anketil, Gunnor, Harald, Ketel, Osmund, Thorgils, Thorketill and many more. The sceptic has only to consult a variety of place-name dictionaries to discover how often the same personal name is attributed to a different nationality.

More important, however, is the fact that the vast majority of Scandinavian place-names in Normandy are hybrids. Thus while in England the names Grim, Björn, Harald, Thor, Guddar and Haco give Grimsby, Burn-thwaite, Harroby, Thoresby, Guttersby and Haconby (-*by* and -*thwaite* being Scandinavian words for a village and a clearing), in Normandy we have Grimonville, Borneville, Hérouville, Tourville, Godarville and Hacque-ville, which suggests that a still Romanized peasantry invented these names by referring to the *villa* (or farm) of Grim, Björn, Harald or the others. As Sir Frank Stenton put it, 'there is no part of Normandy in which, as in many parts of Yorkshire and Lincolnshire, large numbers of local names were created by men speaking a Scandinavian language'.[4] In other words, the lords could have been Scandinavian, but the peasants not. What we have to envisage is conquering Northmen who stepped into the shoes of the Franks as lords of the manor in many villages, drawing their rents and dues from a native peasantry whose language was neither Frankish nor Scandinavian, but French.

William of Jumièges has a story about a peasants' revolt at the beginning of Duke Richard II's reign (996). In the circumstances we have suggested this would hardly have been surprising, but it has sometimes been held that because the peasants organized themselves through local meetings, each of which sent delegates to a central assembly (*conventum*), these peasants 'must' have been Scandinavian. That was certainly not the suggestion of William of Jumièges. The point of his story was that Raoul, Count of Ivry, the Duke's half-brother, showed sense and judgment in the way he suppressed the rebellion. He caught the delegates, cut off their hands and feet, and sent them home as an example to their fellows, who promptly 'forgot their meetings and returned to their ploughs'.[5]

More positively, Professor Musset has been able to show that there was a very real continuity between the estates of the Carolingians and Normans. The large Carolingian estates which can be identified, those of the King and the monasteries, were not broken up at the time of the Norman settlement but were taken over by the Duke in their entirety. Thus when the Duke had become Christian and wanted to restore some of the former monasteries, he was able both to identify their former estates and to

23

return some of them to the newly reconstituted abbeys. The endowment of parish churches was supposed, according to ninth-century regulations, to be a minimum of twelve 'bonniers' of land, and there is evidence to suggest that this was still accepted by the Norman dukes of the eleventh century. The fragmentation of estates and holdings was not greater but less in Normandy than in *Francia* as a whole, and the complicated social divisions of the Carolingian peasantry seem to have resisted the generalizations of feudal nomenclature rather longer in Normandy than elsewhere.[6]

The basic continuity underlying the upheaval of the Norman settlement is clear even in the place-names of the duchy, because those with Scandinavian elements, striking though they may be, are in a minority. Their general distribution is shown on the map opposite, and it will be seen at once that they lie thickest in the Pays de Caux (between Rouen and the sea) and in the northern part of the Cotentin. The map may be misleading round Bayeux, where there is much dispute as to whether the Germanic names are Saxon or Scandinavian, but otherwise the general impression which it gives, even though it shows no more than a selection of names, is a fair reflection of the total distribution. But even within those districts, such as the Pays de Caux, where the Scandinavian names are most pronounced, they are outnumbered by formations which contain no Scandinavian element at all, e.g. Montivilliers (*monasterium villare*), Mortemer (*mortuum mare*), Neufbos (*novum boscum*), Neufmarché (*novum mercatum*) and Neuville (*nova villa*). All the Roman cities have preserved their Latin names in one form or another; Avranches, Bayeux, Evreux and Lisieux were the cities of the *Abrincatui*, *Baiocasses*, *Ebroici* and *Lexovii*, while Coutances was *Constantia*, Rouen *Ratomagus* and Lillebonne *Juliobona*, the capital of the province.

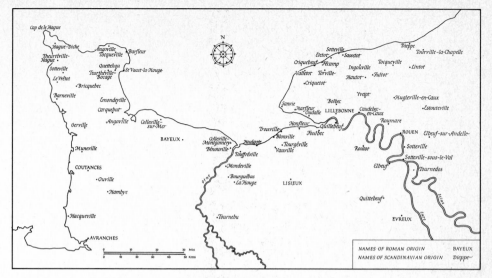

9 Some Scandinavian place-names in Normandy.

It is a remarkable fact that while all these cities preserve Roman remains, sometimes on a very large scale, and the archaeological evidence for the Roman occupation is abundant, the tangible remains of the Northmen in Normandy are sparse. The Hague Dike near Cap de la Hogue in the Cotentin is a fortification which may be Viking – it was apparently built to defend the peninsula against the landsmen – and some isolated objects have been found elsewhere, such as the Viking sword dredged from the Seine at Rouen, but in general the finds are most disappointing. It is possible that if the immigrants were assimilated into the native population rapidly, as is indeed suggested by the coin-hoard of *c.* 970–90 which was discovered at Fécamp in 1965, there would be little chance of discovering objects which were recognizably Scandinavian. But it is hard to believe that even the first generation of immigrants abandoned its native burial customs, and it may be significant that, so far, only one burial has been found which is incontestably Scandinavian.

25

10 This brooch, found at Pitres in 1865, comes from the only undisputedly Scandinavian grave to have been found so far in Normandy.

11 Rollo and his descendants. Dukes of Normandy are shown in capitals.

The evidence against a massive repopulation of Normandy from Scandinavia in the tenth century is overwhelming. It is, however, also indisputable that the Scandinavian Northmen conquered the province and became its lords, and it is important to try and establish whether they attempted to remain a class apart. The test of this would be whether they married among themselves exclusively or also with members of the Frankish aristocracy, but the only family for which we have any evidence relating to the tenth century is that of the dukes. They seem to have married freely with non-Scandinavians. Rollo was said to have married the daughter of the Frankish king and to have had his son by the daughter of a Frankish count. That son, William, married the daughter of a Frankish count and had his son, Richard, by a Breton. None of the dukes' wives came from Scandinavia or England, and by the first half of the eleventh century their family connections were typically French.

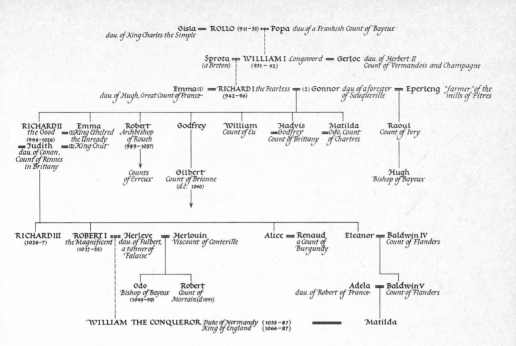

The importance of this conclusion is that it was only in the eleventh century, when the Normans were no longer Scandinavian, that they began to acquire their most Norman characteristics. The great families like the Beaumonts, Bohuns or Warennes emerged in the eleventh century. So did the great abbeys. So did the distinctive style of Norman art and architecture. So did the Normans' consciousness of themselves in literature or history. Whichever way we turn we have to admit that the Viking society of Rollo and his companions was something quite different from the Norman society of the eleventh century. The one developed from the other, but the development was not effective until the two races had merged and the Northmen had, for all practical purposes, become Frenchmen.

What was it then that made the Normans different? The first and most obvious reason was that they had a relatively well organized state and an extremely powerful army

27

which enabled the Norman dukes to play an influential part in the politics of North-West Europe. Whatever one might think of the Normans as a race, no one could ignore them as a power; and they themselves were bound to appreciate the advantages and profitability of such a situation. It is important, therefore, to see what were the factors which made their government and their army so strong.

The duke's government was strong because he exercised many of the prerogatives of the Frankish kings.[7] When Charles the Simple granted the province to Rollo, he probably granted it as a march (or frontier province), bestowing many of his own powers on the marquis or duke, so that he could defend the territory effectively. In a military sense Normandy was the natural defensive zone covering the Seine valley from the west. From Lower Normandy, especially the district round Bayeux and Caen, there was an easy approach to Paris, and it was vital to defend it against both the Bretons and maritime invaders. It was worth while for the king to delegate royal powers to any marquis or duke who could accomplish this task effectively.

Normandy was not the only such march or duchy to be created by the Frankish kings. There were several of them, including Flanders, Anjou, Aquitaine and Burgundy, and they all developed into territorial principalities. Normandy emerged stronger than most, because the Norman dukes were ruthless in sweeping away the Frankish nobility which in most other districts proved the bane of strong government. In Normandy the nobles were unable to convert the *pagi* into hereditary counties; the duke controlled them through his viscounts, who collected such taxes as there were, did justice and had the custody of the duke's castles. Above all the duke was incomparably richer than any of his nobles. At the beginning of the eleventh

12 Carved runestone from Swedish Gotland showing a primitive Viking ship. This is the art of the Northmen before they became Normans.

13 Norman victories were not won by personal valour alone. This illustration from the Bayeux Tapestry shows how proud the Normans were of their military equipment.

century, when we begin to have some solid information, it is clear that the duke held the lion's share of the former royal demesne, the lion's share of the land of those religious houses which had become defunct and had not yet been refounded, and the monopoly of the mint. He was probably as rich as any territorial prince in the whole Frankish kingdom.

The Norman dukes, unlike some other territorial princes, used their wealth to reorganize their army. The traditional Viking force of light cavalry organized by ship-loads had not been designed for set battles but for lightning raids, which would plunder towns or monasteries and disappear with the booty before an army could be put in the field against them. The needs of defence and regular warfare were very different, and it was probably not much before the second or third decade of the eleventh century that the Normans had made the necessary adaptations, but then we begin to hear a lot about their military exploits. They intervened successfully in Burgundy, were largely

14 The Normans boasted that they built the fleet for the invasion of England in eight months.

responsible for the restoration in turn of King Henry I of France and Count Baldwin IV of Flanders, and campaigned successfully against the Bretons.

They were very conscious of their military prowess and sometimes liked to think that their victories were due solely to their fighting spirit; William of Jumièges has a splendid tale of some luckless English raiders who discovered, to their cost, that even the women of Normandy were bonny fighters when they laid about them with the yokes of their milk-pails, but this sort of story did less than justice to the time, effort and money which the Normans spent on military training and military equipment. They were prepared to spend a fortune on horses, armour, castles and (if necessary) ships. It was typical that in the Bayeux Tapestry a major feature was made of the organization of supplies – helmets, hauberks, swords, lances, axes and barrels and skins of wine – and of the building of the fleet, which was apparently completed in eight months. The Normans undoubtedly found war profitable, but they ploughed their profits back into the business. According to Anna Comnena, the one thing that Bohemond said when he was shown the treasure-store of the Byzantine Emperor was: 'If I had such wealth I would long ago have become master of many lands.'[8]

In the eleventh century the most important element in any army was its knights, and the essence of a knight was that he fought on horseback. Consequently the most important item of his equipment was a horse. It had to be a horse of a very special sort. A draught horse would have been too cumbersome, and a palfrey unable to bear the weight of the knight's armour. What was needed was a horse which was specially bred for strength and speed, which could manœuvre easily, and which was trained not to panic in battle. Such a horse was called a destrier, apparently because it was led by the squire with his right hand, and was enormously expensive, about thirty times the cost of a palfrey. We know surprisingly little about the breeding of destriers, but the Normans had enough money to buy plenty of them, and were clearly connoisseurs of what they bought. One of the most impressive features of the Bayeux Tapestry is the pride and joy which its artists took in depicting horses. We are given an individual portrait of the Duke's extremely virile horse (Pl. 15), and can recognize it again in other scenes. We are shown horses galloping (Pl. 16), horses tossing their heads, horses enjoying the sea-trip (Pl. 17), horses disembarking at Pevensey (Pl. 18), and of course horses in battle (Pls. 19, 20). In the battle scenes it is made to look as if every Norman were part of a horse and that the number of horses was legion. So far from being given the impression that the battle was won against odds, one is shown that the resources of the Normans were so overwhelming that no one could possibly defeat them.

15, 16 Horses were the most important items of military equipment. *Opposite:* William the Conqueror's charger at Hastings, apparently of the Andalusian breed; Wace tells a story of how it had been sent to William from Spain. *Below:* two messengers at the gallop.

EXIERVNT:DEhESTENGA:

NVNTII:VVILLELMI

17–20 The artists of the Bayeux Tapestry delighted in depicting horses. Here they are shown (*top*) crossing the Channel and apparently enjoying the view, and (*above*) disembarking at Pevensey; (*right, top*) in the thick of battle (note the inscription referring to English and 'French'); and (*right*) in pursuit of the fleeing English.

The management of horses was as important as the horses themselves. This had long been recognized, and in the ninth century it was already a proverb that a horseman could be made of a lad at puberty, but later than that never. The more complicated the manœuvres expected, and the more use that was made of the lance and the shock-charge, the more expert that training had to be. William of Apulia, when he contrasted the Normans with the Germans in Italy, said that though the Germans were splendid fighters on foot, they were 'not very sure in the management of their horses' and that they struck harder with the sword than the lance because their horses were 'not trained to turn at the touch of their hands'.[9] In northern France the art was more highly developed than elsewhere, and among the northern French the Normans seem to have been pre-eminent. Otherwise it would be hard to explain why they were in such demand as mercenaries in Italy, or so outstanding among the warriors of the First Crusade.

In war nothing succeeds like success, and as soon as the Normans had acquired a reputation for victory they attracted expert recruits from neighbouring countries, in much the same way as nowadays the best football teams have the least difficulty in attracting the best players. In the first quarter of the eleventh century a considerable number of Frenchmen and Bretons were recruited in this way and were rewarded with grants of land. Among those who were Frankish or French were the Bellêmes and the counts of the Vexin; the Giroies were half-French and half-Breton; the Paiens of Gisors came probably from Touraine and the Tessons from Anjou, while the father of Baudri de Bocquencé was a German (*Teutonicus*) who had migrated to Normandy to serve under Duke Richard. As we shall presently see, Dudo (writing in the 1020s) took it for granted that the knights of the Norman dukes would have been recruited from many different peoples. William the Conqueror was only following the accepted policy of his predecessors when he recruited knights from Brittany, Flanders, Artois and Picardy, for his invasion of England.

In England we are so used to the names of those families who 'came over with the Conqueror' – de Beaumont, de Montfort, de Montgomery and the like – that we tend to assume that at that date they were already ancient and well established in Normandy. In fact they were nearly all new in the sense that whether they were immigrants or, like Roger de Montgomery, *ex Northmannis Northmannus*, it was only rarely that they had acquired the lands from which they took their family name before the 1030s. The very earliest case known is that of de Tosny whose surname is first recorded in 1014. Tosny (which is across the Seine from Les Andelys) had formed part of the estates of the archbishopric of Rouen, but shortly before 990 it was given by Archbishop Hugh, who was a Frenchman and former monk of Saint-Denis, to his brother Ralph, who promptly called himself 'de Tosny', thus establishing himself at one stroke as a Norman and a noble.[10]

It is the emergence of this new nobility which marks the real break between what we might describe as the sub-Carolingian period and the real Normandy. The new nobility cannot be traced back to the Carolingian period in any way. In the twelfth century those who claimed to be 'genuine' Normans might produce some rather hopeful genealogies, but none of them carries conviction, and historians have been forced to conclude that the nobles of the eleventh century did not themselves know anything about their remoter ancestry. For them the tenth century was as much a 'dark age' as it is for us.

Much the same pattern can be seen in the history of the Church, even though the creation of the duchy had a lasting effect on it. The boundaries of the duchy were almost identical with those of the archbishop's province, with the result that Normandy and the ecclesiastical province became merely two aspects of what was virtually the same territory. This put the duke in a commanding position, and it is not surprising that he used it to the full. Archbishop Robert (989–1037) was a son of Duke Richard I, and Archbishop Malger (1037–54) of Richard II, and people referred, as historians still do, to 'the Norman Church' rather than 'the province of Rouen', because that was the reality. In it the duke was all-important.

In the tenth century the Norman Church was still in its 'dark age'.[11] Under the later Carolingians it had suffered greatly from the raids of the Northmen (who, among other things, were responsible for the deaths of the bishops of Bayeux and Coutances in 858 and 889 respectively), from the Bretons (to whom in 867 King Charles the Bald had surrendered the territories, if not the bishoprics, of Avranches, Coutances and Bayeux), and from the Frankish aristocracy (who, in the guise of 'protectors', often succeeded in purloining those estates which the invaders had spared). In face of these perils many bishops and clergy had either fled or disappeared. Rouen remained relatively safe for the archbishops, but they were joined there by five successive bishops of Coutances who apparently did not dare to live in their own diocese between 913 and c. 1025. At other sees there are simply gaps in the lists of bishops, at Avranches from 862 to 990, at Bayeux from 876 to 930, at Lisieux from 832 to 990, and at Sées from 910 to 936. It may be that there were bishops during these periods, but the disorganization of the sees was such that their names were not recorded.

The monasteries almost disappeared from view. During the period of the Northmen's raids the monks had often fled from their abbeys and removed their most precious

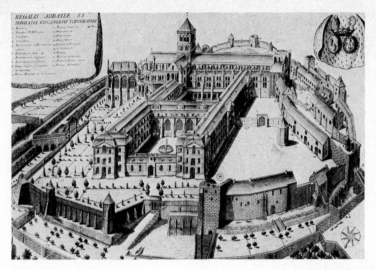

21 The abbey of Fécamp as it appeared in 1687. This can be compared with the fifteenth-century picture (Pl. 30).

relics to places of safety.[12] At first they would have hoped to come back as soon as the danger was past, and sometimes they did; but eventually they stayed away too long and found it impossible to return. The monks of Jumièges had fled to Haspres, and those of Fontanelle to Chartres, Boulogne and eventually, *Blandinium* near Ghent. But wherever they went, they or their successors kept the memory of the monastery alive and eventually returned, to Jumièges by 940 and to Fontanelle (Saint-Wandrille) in 961. It is a surprising fact that after these migrations they succeeded in recovering a part at least of their original endowments, in the case of Jumièges by the gift of Duke William Longsword who must have restored the lands in the immediate vicinity of the abbey by 940 at latest. Other restorations in the tenth century were at Mont-Saint-Michel (though this abbey may never have been totally deserted), Saint-Ouen and Fécamp, but the monastic life was at best mediocre and some houses were, like Fécamp, in fact colleges of secular clerks.

39

22 *Opposite:* nave of the abbey church of Mont-Saint-Michel. The north side (here shown) was restored after 1103 but follows the general design of the south side (1023–48).

23 Ruins of the church of St Pierre at Jumièges. On the far wall can be seen the outline of the arches of the west end of the nave as it was rebuilt in the tenth century after the monks had returned from their 'exile'.

24 West front of the large church of Notre Dame at Jumièges, which replaced the smaller tenth-century church in 1067.

The decisive change was in 1001 when Duke Richard II decided to replace the secular clerks at Fécamp with a monastic community. Having no distinguished monks within the duchy he looked abroad, as he had also done in his search for knights, and succeeded in attracting a noted reformer called William of Volpiano. William was an Italian but he had been trained at Cluny and had subsequently effected a widespread reform of monasteries in the region of Dijon, where he was Abbot of Saint-Bénigne. Once he was installed at Fécamp his influence became widespread. He brought about reforms at Jumièges, Mont-Saint-Michel and Saint-Ouen, and founded dependent monasteries at Saint-Taurin d'Evreux, Montivilliers and Bernay. He and his successor, John of Ravenna (another Italian and a nephew of his), played an important part in the reconversion and reorganization of the dioceses of Bayeux and Coutances by acquiring estates and establishing parish churches in them, and by assisting in the foundation of new monasteries at Troarn, Saint-Martin-du-Bosc and Saint-Gabriel.

In this way the work of William of Volpiano had the widest possible effects on the religious life of the Norman Church. The number of monasteries increased rapidly. In 1000 there had only been five in the duchy, but by 1035 the number had grown to ten, and by 1066 to thirty at least. Those founded before 1035 all owed their origin to the Duke or members of his family, but after 1035 it was the new nobility which provided the most benefactors. As Orderic put it, 'each magnate would have thought himself beneath contempt if he had not supported clerks on his estate for the service of God.'[13]

In one sense the foundation of a monastery was a feudal investment; it linked a man with his estates as closely as any castle, since it was there that he would be buried, there that masses would be said for his soul, and there that his name would be remembered for ever. But there can be no doubt that the movement started by William of Volpiano sparked off a genuine religious reform. Even the bishops (a worldly lot belonging to the new aristocracy) were moved to reorganize their dioceses. It was in the middle years of the eleventh century that archdeaconries were established for the supervision and control of the parish clergy in most dioceses, and in those years also that regular cathedral chapters were instituted, with a dean and canons, precentor and master of the schools.

As in war, so in religion, nothing succeeds like success, and once the reform movement had started, it attracted further talent from abroad. Isembard, the learned Abbot of the Holy Trinity at Rouen (1030–51), was a German, and so also was Ainard, the first Abbot of Saint-Pierre-sur-Dives (1046–78). By far the most important of the foreign recruits, however, was an Italian called Lanfranc. He was attracted to Normandy in the first place because he had heard that there was a lack of learning there, and that as a teacher he might expect to gain wealth and honour there. He arrived in 1039 and for a couple of years taught at Avranches – itself a striking tribute to ecclesiastical reorganization – but subsequently became a monk at the poorest monastery he could find. This was Bec, a house which had been founded by one of the lesser members of the new nobility, called Herluin, in order that he might himself renounce the world and become a monk there. Lanfranc joined him (c. 1041–2) and after about three years set up a school in the monastery, which immediately transformed it from a place of obscurity into one of the most famous abbeys of Europe. Pupils flocked to it from France, Gascony, Brittany, Flanders, Germany and Italy, the most notable being two Italians, Anselm of Lucca, the future Pope Alexander II (1061–73), and Anselm of Aosta, who was to prove himself one of the greatest intellects of the Middle Ages. He had come to Bec in 1059, specifically to sit at Lanfranc's feet, but though this had not been his original intention he soon entered the monastery, becoming prior (1063) and abbot (1078) before being nominated by William II to succeed Lanfranc as Archbishop of Canterbury (1093).

With such men as Lanfranc and Anselm becoming Norman monks it was only to be expected that the whole picture of Normandy should be changed from a land of outlandish barbarism to one where conspicuous wealth was placed at the disposal of religion, the arts and culture generally. By the 1050s and 1060s new abbey churches were being built at Mont-Saint-Michel, Bernay, Jumièges and Caen, displaying the beginnings of the distinctively Norman style of architecture which was to reach its apogee in Norman England. The churchmen of Normandy had attained a wide reputation as reformers, even if their style of reform was not in the Hildebrandine tradition; their scholars were among the finest in Europe, and their dukes were known as magnificent patrons.

It was a far cry from the Scandinavian origins, and though it can be claimed that the Scandinavian element was 'the little leaven that leaveneth the lump', the plain fact was that in the eleventh century Normandy was a territorial principality with a new aristocracy, a new Church, a new monasticism and a new culture. The dukes had recruited conspicuous talent from abroad, choosing the best wherever it might be found – knights from France and monks from Italy – and as a result they had produced a new state and a new society, which no longer belonged to the Scandinavian world, but was in the forefront of the military and cultural development of the French.

25 Twelfth-century manuscript from the abbey of Bec, with a commentary on Luke 10, 38–9.

N ILLO t̄ : Intrauit ihs inquodam castellum &
mulier quedam martha nomine excepit illu in
domū suam. Et huic erat soror: nomine maria. Et a

A multis solet queri cur hoc sm̄ euangl̄m inso
lennitate assūptionis beate ui genitricis
inecclesiis ui p orbē legat̄. cū nil adeam inipso
ppe ptinē uideat̄. Scdm̄ ē. qd scī patresq̄ ecclesiastica
officia statuerc̄ non sine certa ratione id constituisse credendi
st̄ quāuis illorū asertio usq; nc̄ nob maneat incognita.
Qb; dā ū uidet̄ idō fuisse statutū. eo qd nulla ppetate
abet h̄ festiuitas inaliq̄ narratione euangeliorū queppr̄e
uideat̄ ptinē adeam. Scī appe euangeliste qi genealogiā
dn̄i & ipsi intemerate genitricis descripserunt. & qi
de ei annunciatione ab anglo facta. & de eius acta
purificatione intemplo & de cetis reb; que adeā ptinent
circa natiuitatē & puericiā dn̄i saluatoris scripserc̄
de ipsi assūptione nichil omnino scripsisse inueniūt.
qd multis mirū uidet̄. Et hoc maxime de iohanne
euangelista qi custos & loco matris eā abuit p passionē
dn̄i. qq; p et transitū multis annis sup uixit ipsius.
sacro transitu p̄hens afuisse credendū ē. nichil lītīs
cō mendasse inuenit̄ de ea n̄ queda uerba que dn̄e cōs̄
xp̄e filius ei inchana galilee aquā mutauit inuinū sua
diuina uirtute & ideo inpassione narrat de illa & deseipso
hoc m̄. stabant aū iuxta crucē iesu mat̄ ei & soror it̄rs
ei maria cleophe & maria magdalene. Cū q̄ uidisset
ihs matrē & disciplm stantē que diligebat. dix̄ matri sue.
mulier. ecce fili tuus. Addiscipulmaā. ecce mat̄ tua. & ex
illa hora. accepit eā discipl's insua. Hoc ē. totu qd ioh s
narrat de ea. Luiaq̄ null euangelistarū qd gesseric p
morte filii sui. nec qn̄ transiertt de hacuita lītīs cōdasse
repperiunt. ideo p hibent fuisse statutū ut hoc euangeliū
insollennitate assūptionis ei legeret. q si subtilit̄ qis in
uestigare uoluerit. plura ineo reperie. que beate marie
p facile aptari possint. Nā inconueniens uidet̄ euangliū
qd narrat q̄tica incarnatione & inipsa solennitate
ut dec̄ā legit̄ si inhac rc̄rū legeret Similit̄ ea que circa
natiuitatē xpi & ei infantiam sūt scripta & diebus legunt̄
si inhac rc̄rū recitarent omino n̄ for̄t actum nec congruum

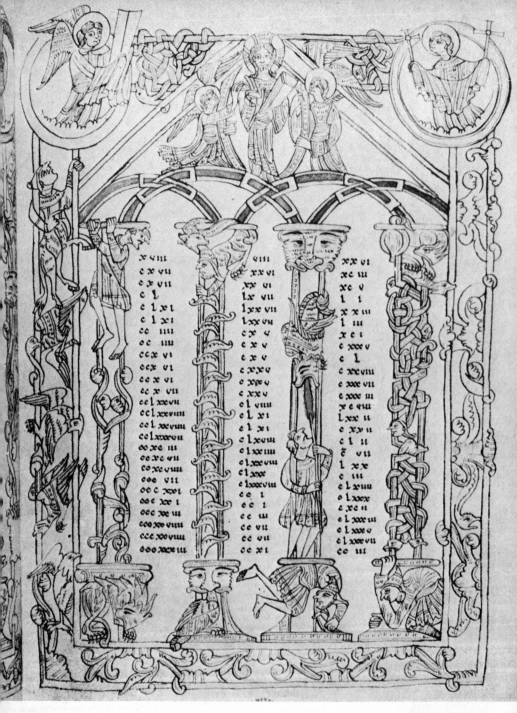

26 Canon tables from the Jumièges Gospels. Though it was written and illuminated at Jumièges, Anglo-Saxon influence is very evident.

27 Jumièges Gospels. St Matthew writing his gospel (*cf*. Pl. 69).

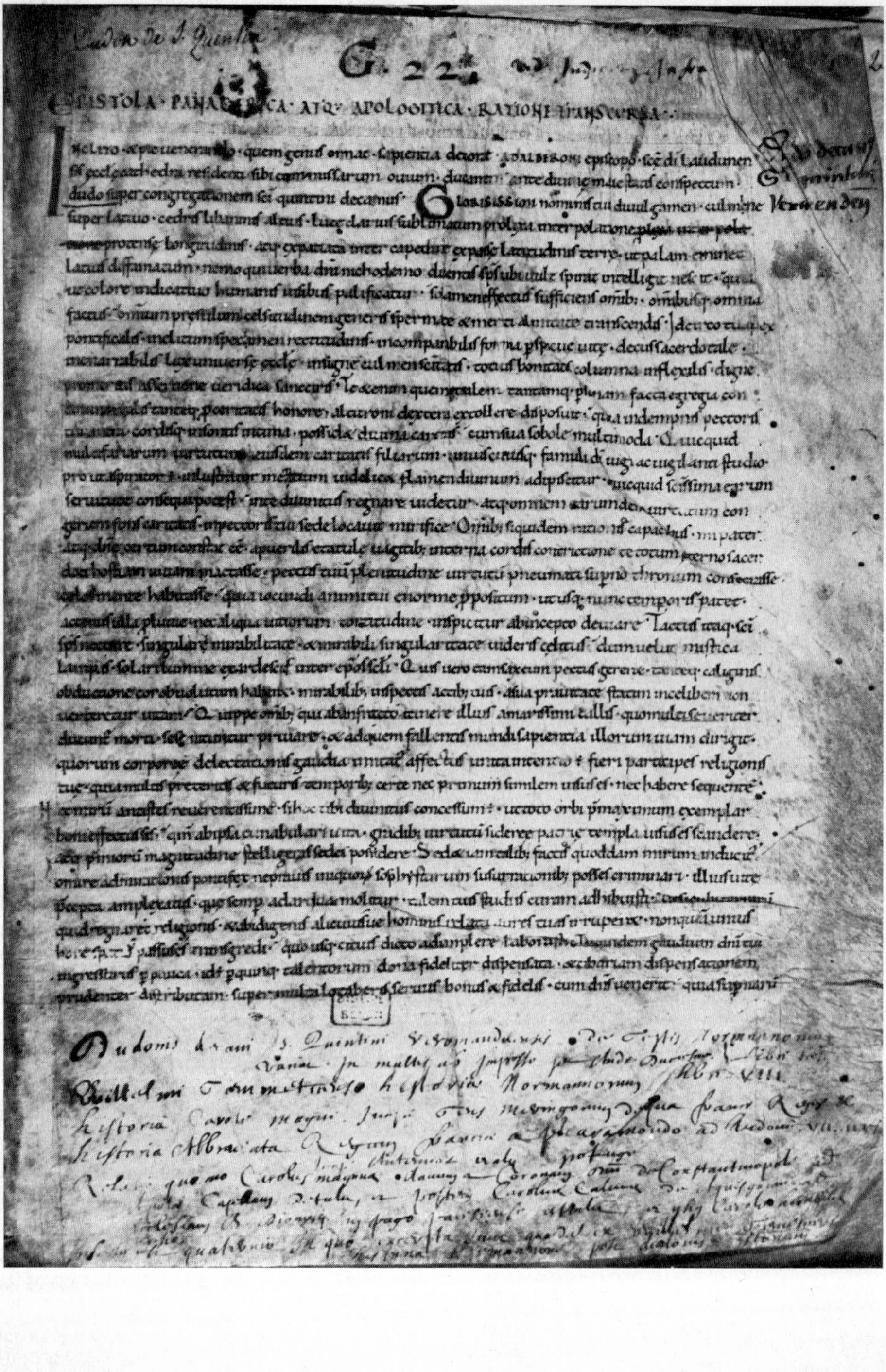

G. 22

EPISTOLA · PANEGYRICA · ATQ· APOLOGETICA · RATIONE · TRANSCURSA ·

[Dense medieval Latin text in insular/caroline minuscule, largely illegible due to fading and condition of the manuscript. The main body consists of a panegyric and apologetic epistle addressed to Adalbero, bishop of Laon.]

[At the foot of the page, later cursive annotations:]

Dudonis decani S. Quentini Veromandorum de Gestis Normannorum ...
Variae in multis ab impresso ... edita Duacensi ... 1619 ...

Willelmi ... cum materie historiae Normannorum ...

Historia Caroli Magni ...

Historia Abbreviata Regum ...

Chapter Two

The Norman myth

We may have grave doubts as to the extent to which the Normans were racially distinct, but we can have no doubt that they believed themselves to be a people. As a general proposition this is not in the least surprising, because it is doubtful if any nation is racially 'pure'; the example of the USA is only the most obvious of many in which nations can be seen to have been formed out of a mixed population. What no nation can be without is an image or myth with which it can identify itself. This image can be provided by legend or history, religion, poetry, folklore, or what we more vaguely call 'tradition'. It need not be expressed in precise or absolute terms; on the contrary it is usually flexible and capable of being gradually transformed, but if a people is to be conscious of its identity it must have such an image, and if we are to understand the Normans, we must discover what theirs was.

There is a considerable amount of material for this study, because the Normans wrote, or commissioned, a number of histories of themselves. Excluding for the moment those written by or about the Normans in Italy, the main items are as follows:

c. 1015–26	Dudo of Saint-Quentin, *De Moribus et Actis Primorum Normanniae Ducum*
c. 1067(?)	The *Carmen de Hastingae Proelio* attributed to Guy of Amiens
1070s	The Bayeux Tapestry
c. 1070–1	William of Jumièges, *Gesta Normannorum Ducum*
c. 1073–4	William of Poitiers, *Gesta Guillelmi*

28 This manuscript of Dudo's history comes from the abbey of Jumièges and may well have been used by William of Jumièges when he was writing his own work.

Considered purely as history, they are of very unequal value, but what concerns us now is not their historical accuracy, but the evidence which they supply for the beliefs and aspirations of the Normans at the date at which they were written.

This point applies with special force to the first work on the list, 'The Manners and Deeds of the First Dukes of Normandy' (*De Moribus et Actis Primorum Normanniae Ducum*) by Dudo of Saint-Quentin.[1] Dudo was not a Norman, but he tells us that he had met Duke Richard I in the last two years of his life (995–6), and had been persuaded by him to undertake the work, but had hardly begun it when the Duke died. He had continued with the aid of Duke Richard II (996–1026), who was still alive when he was writing, and had received much information from that Duke's half-brother Raoul, Count of Ivry, but he had evidently not finished writing by 1015, because in his preface he styles himself dean (rather than canon) of

Saint-Quentin.[2] There has been a certain amount of controversy (some of it rather ridiculous) as to how much, if any, of the work should be regarded as history, but since it was written for the Duke, we can assume that it attempts to express what the Duke *wanted* to believe about his predecessors.

What makes Dudo's work quite exceptionally fascinating is that the way in which it was used by later writers enables us to detect which parts of it had the greatest appeal for subsequent generations. In 1070–1 an updated compendium of it was composed by William of Jumièges, and new editions of this, each with its own interpolations, were produced by an anonymous monk of Caen soon after 1087, by Orderic Vitalis before 1109, and by Robert de Torigni *c.* 1142–50. Shortly afterwards Wace and Benoît drew on all this previous material for their long narrative poems, the *Roman de Rou* (Rollo) (*c.* 1160–74) and the *Chronique des Ducs de Normandie* (*c.* 1172–6) which, being written in Old French, were both intended for secular audiences. The result is something like a theme with variations, each successive editor or author making slight changes of accent or tone, and introducing new subsidiary material, which all builds up to a grand restatement and finale. We are, therefore, in a position to undertake an interesting historical exercise. Normally when a historian studies texts he is anxious to remove later accretions so as to discover what was originally stated. In this case the original statement is not in dispute, and our interest will be focused on the way in which different aspects of it did, or did not, become magnified or transformed when passed on from one generation to another.

Dudo's *De Moribus et Actis Primorum Normanniae Ducum* is a rambling and verbose book of inordinate literary pretensions and with many apostrophes in verse. It relates the story of the origin of the Normans and of

51

their first three dukes, Rollo (911–31), William Long-sword (931–42) and Richard I (942–96), and its purpose was obviously to demonstrate that by the end of the tenth century the Normans had shed their bad Viking qualities and become good Christian citizens. The francization of the Normans is, therefore, its main theme, but its tone is defensive. Duke Richard I had evidently shocked Western society by summoning a host of pagan pirates from Denmark to help him in his struggle against King Lothair. Dudo defended him vigorously, insisting that he had been driven to make this dangerous alliance because of the consistent hostility and bad faith of the King, and that he had subsequently taken care to convert his pagan allies by preaching to them in person for sixteen days on end. Of Richard's virtues Dudo had no doubt; he illustrated them by reference to the beatitudes and ended with a glowing description of the monastery he had founded at Fécamp. Indeed one would almost think that Dudo had not realized the difference between hagiography and bio-graphy, because he endeavoured to give an aura of holiness to the first three dukes which is, to say the least, unconvinc-ing. He tells us at length how William Longsword had set his heart on being a monk, he treats his murder as a martyrdom, and he insists that Rollo, though a pagan till 911, had been led to the conquest of Normandy by the will of God, as it had been revealed to him in a vision.

In this vision, says Dudo, Rollo found himself on a high mountain in *Francia*. At the top of the mountain was a wondrous spring in which he bathed, thus curing himself of an itching leprosy. Remaining on the mountain, he saw that all around its base were birds of divers kinds and divers colours, except that they all had red left wings. The birds stretched as far as the eye could see, but they approached the mountain top in turn and bathed in the spring in an orderly manner. When they had all bathed, they arranged themselves without distinction of kind or sort and fed together in amity without quarrelling. Then they fetched twigs, built nests, and at Rollo's command lay down in them.

It hardly needs to be explained (though Dudo made a Christian captive do so) that the mountain signified the Church, Rollo's bathing his baptism, and the building of nests the rebuilding of the walls of the towns which the Northmen had destroyed. But the birds are interesting. We are told that they were of different kinds and different colours because Rollo's subjects were to come from various countries, and that their red left wings denoted the shields which they would wear in his service. The conclusion that 'as the birds of different kinds obeyed you, so men of divers nations will serve you and lie down at your behest' suggests that even in the 1020s it was necessary to explain how it was that, racially speaking, the Normans were such a mixed bag.[3]

Dudo did not mind stating that the Duke's subjects were not all Danes, because his primary aim was to establish that it was God who had led Rollo to France, and that he had done so in order that he might be converted not only to Christianity, but also to Frankish civilization. Hence the emphasis which he put not only on Rollo's baptism, but also on his marriage to the daughter of King Charles the Simple; not only on the monastic ambition of William Longsword, but also on the fact that he was half-French (*patre Daco matre Francigena*) and had to defeat a formidable rebellion of those Normans who complained of his French relatives, his French friends and his French manners; not only on Duke Richard's preaching to the Danes, but also on the fact that, in spite of his alliance with the heathen, he had been trying throughout to behave like an ordinary French magnate if only the King would recognize him as such.

This 'French' thesis of Dudo's at first had a very great success, so much so that until the end of the eleventh century most Normans were indifferent to whether they called themselves Norman or French, using the words *Galli* or *Franci* as synonyms for *Normanni*.[4] But in the course of time there was a reaction against this assimilation. It is first found in William of Jumièges, but in general it belongs to the twelfth century rather than the eleventh, and is obvious from the way in which writers use the terms *Franci* and *Normanni* as antonyms. In one sense this is strange, because in fact the Normans were even more French in the twelfth century than they had been in the eleventh. But the more French they became, the more desperate they were to establish their identity, laying more and more stress on their Danish ancestry and the heroic deeds of Hasting and Rollo in the days when they really had been 'different'. It was a nostalgic sentiment, but not so much a negation of the previous attitude as a change of emphasis. Dudo had insisted that though the Normans were Danish they had become French; William of Jumièges and the twelfth-century writers, that though the Normans were French they were different because basically they were still Norman.

In Dudo the original Danishry of the Normans was expressed most fully in his first book, where it could not possibly conflict with his 'French' thesis, since it was concerned with the Northmen before Rollo, and particularly with Hasting. Hasting was neither a duke of Normandy nor an ancestor of Rollo, but simply the archetypal Northman. The features which characterized him were not the 'Nordic' qualities favoured by romantic historians, but ferocity and cunning. According to Dudo, he got tired of pillaging *Francia* and determined to sack Rome, but went to the wrong place and besieged a city called Luna. When he found it heavily defended, he spun a yarn about having been expelled from *Francia* and said that all he wanted was to be baptized. After baptism he pretended to take ill and die. On his instructions, his companions begged leave to bury him in the minster and carried him into the city on a bier, but just as he was about to be lowered into the grave he jumped up, strangled the bishop and turned his men loose on the city. Thinking that he had captured the capital of the world he was delighted with his achievement but when he discovered that the place was not Rome but Luna his fury knew no bounds. He despoiled the whole province and returned to *Francia*.[5]

Despite the resemblance of this story to that of the Trojan horse (and Dudo specifically states that the Danes boasted of their descent from the Trojan Antenor[6]) some historians have tried to find a grain of truth in it, to identify Luna and date the raid, but for us its sole significance lies in the fact that it became one of the most popular stories of the Norman myth. Not only was it repeated by William of Jumièges, by all his editors, and by Wace and Benoît, but the idea of being carried through the enemy lines in a coffin was to become the basis of a whole series of stories about the Normans in Italy. Anna Comnena, who was writing in Byzantium in the 1140s (but is thought to have had access to a Norman *chanson de geste*), tells a similar story about Bohemond's escape from Antioch (1105), adding as a refinement that a dead cock was put with him in the coffin so that the smell should suggest that his body was in a state of 'rare putrefaction'. Later in the twelfth century Otto of Freising tells how Roger of Sicily captured Corfu by a similar ruse, and in the thirteenth century the story was applied by Snorri Sturluson to Harald Hardrada in Sicily, and by Matthew Paris to Robert Guiscard's capture of Monte Cassino.[7]

When Dudo wrote of Rollo himself, the Danish attribute on which he laid most stress was not so much cunning (though that is not lacking) as a refusal to accept anyone as his lord. In one story this characteristic came close to the idea of the Danish free warrior. When, in the parley with Alsting, Rollo's men were asked the name of their lord (*senior*), they replied, 'None, because we are all equal.'[8] It was a story which had a great appeal and was repeated throughout the twelfth century. William of Jumièges seems to be the only writer who found it puzzling. In order to reconcile the statement with the fact that these men were clearly under the command of Rollo, he added a passage to explain that the exigencies of the siege of Paris had forced the Danes to choose a leader, and that they had then chosen Rollo by lot – a brave attempt to explain how these free warriors had come to have a hereditary duke.[9]

Most Norman writers, however, interpreted the claim to have no lord as a rejection of Frankish overlordship. This theme also was to be found in Dudo. In his story of the treaty of Saint-Claire-sur-Epte, he said that the King gave Rollo 'the land as it had been determined from the Epte to the sea as an alod [*in alodo et in fundo*]'.

Then the bishops said: 'Anyone who receives such a gift ought to bend down and kiss the King's foot.' But Rollo said: 'Never will I bend my knees to anyone else's knees, nor will I kiss anyone's foot.' But impelled by the entreaties of the Franks he ordered a certain soldier to kiss the King's foot; and he immediately took hold of the King's foot, lifted it up to his mouth and, still standing, kissed it, thus toppling the King over.[10]

Subsequently, at a second treaty of Saint-Claire-sur-Epte, Dudo made King Louis IV confirm Normandy to Duke Richard I 'so that he and his succession might hold it and possess it, and render service to no one but God'.[11] For good measure, he made the King say:

The land of Normandy will never be defended unless it is under the protection of one lord; and it ought not to be divided, since it is properly a whole. . . . The Danish people can serve only one lord.[12]

This brings us to Dudo's third theme, which was that the land of Normandy was a unity and indivisible. It was called Normandy because it belonged to the Normans, but conversely the Normans belonged to it. It was on the land of Normandy that Dudo's patriotism was centred. He insisted on its fertility, was eloquent about the blue waters (*gurgite caeruleo*) of the Seine, described how they lapped 'the odoriferous grasses of its bank' and apostrophized the city of Rouen five times in verse. He was careful to attach stories to particular places so that in Rouen, for example, at St Martin's Church the landing of Rollo would be recalled, at Le Pré-de-la-Bataille William Longsword's victory over the rebels, at the ducal hall (*domum principum civitatis illius*) the attempt of Louis IV to capture the little Duke Richard, at the Beauvais gate the death of Otto I's nephew, and at the church of Saint-Ouen Otto I's decision to retreat from Normandy, and so on. Outside Rouen his knowledge was meagre, but Longpaon was associated with Rollo's famous judgment on the husbandman who allowed his wife to steal his plough, Pont de l'Arche with the Danish camp at *As Dans*, and Jeufosse with Duke Richard's preaching to his pagan allies. The history of the Normans was shown to be deeply rooted in the soil of Normandy.

This was a most important part of the Norman myth. Once it was accepted that the Normans were not wholly Danish or wholly French, but were (like the birds of Rollo's dream) immigrants from a whole variety of countries, the one thing which made a man Norman was his attachment to Normandy. It was not a very difficult concept in an age in which it was the normal thing for a knight, as soon as he had acquired an estate, to adopt its name as his surname, but it had a wider application than is sometimes recognized. Orderic Vitalis, the greatest of Norman historians, was born in England. His mother was English and his father a French priest in the service of a Norman lord, but at the age of ten he was sent to Normandy to become a monk of Saint-Evroul. Thereafter he had two patriotisms. Though he proudly called himself 'English-born' (*Angligena*) and viewed Duke William's conquest of England with bitterness, he had no doubt that he was a Norman monk and belonged to Normandy.

It was perhaps because of this paradox that he put such stress on the antiquity of Normandy. It was only a short step from believing that people were made Norman because they lived in Normandy, to endowing that country with a personality; and to believing that if it had a personality, it must always have existed, even before the arrival of 'its' people. This certainly was what Orderic Vitalis believed, and he expressed it in his concept of *Neustria*. Though originally used in the ninth century for a far larger area between the Loire and the Seine, the term *Neustria* had become a high-sounding synonym for Normandy, at any rate from the end of the eleventh century.[13] Orderic used it, however, not as a literary ornament, but functionally as the name for pre-Norman Normandy. He needed such a name because the history he was writing was primarily ecclesiastical, and he could not possibly escape the fact that the Norman Church had a considerable history in the pre-Norman period. How was he to establish the continuity of Norman bishoprics, or explain the origin of monasteries such as his own, unless he explained their prehistory? And if he did that, it was almost impossible not to project the whole of Normandy into the past and write, as he did, about 'the region once called *Neustria* and now Normandy'.[14]

When the history of a people develops into the history of a land, it almost inevitably becomes teleological. The land is represented as having a destiny or, in religious terms, as having been promised by God to a chosen people. The most famous example is in the Old Testament, but whether expressed or implied, the idea is fundamental to the concept of a nation. No people can be a nation unless it can project itself into timelessness by linking its history to a particular land, and it has no chance of doing that unless it believes the link to be true. That is why nations are so often said to be 'gaining consciousness' of themselves, as if they had always been in existence though unconscious of the fact. In the case of Normandy, Dudo had been the first to suggest, in the story of Rollo's dream, that God had destined the land for the Normans, but it was Orderic who worked out the historical implications and convinced his readers that under some name or other Normandy had always been a distinct and natural entity.

29 *Above:* Fifteenth-century illustration of the marriage of Duke Rollo to Gisla, daughter of King Charles the Simple. This and the following three pictures come from a manuscript made for a Burgundian nobleman soon after 1481.

30–2 Fifteenth-century illustrations of (*above*) Duke Richard I at the
building of the abbey of Fécamp; (*opposite, top*) the murder of William
Longsword who is shown twice, parleying with Arnold Count of
Flanders, and being murdered; (*opposite, below*) Rollo landing at St Martin's
gate in Rouen. In all these pictures the costume and architecture are those
of the fifteenth century.

60

Logic and consistency are not necessarily the strongest features of a national myth. In the case of the Norman myth, not only was the French theme balanced against a Danish theme, but the Normandy theme was balanced by a theme of wider conquest. Normandy was not enough for the Normans; they wanted to make conquests everywhere, and already in Dudo they were beginning to make larger claims. The first was to Brittany, Dudo's story being that when Rollo was granted Normandy he found it so devastated, 'untilled by the plough, stripped of all beasts and cattle, and rendered useless to men', that he had also to be given 'the whole of Brittany off which to live'.[15] In consequence Dudo referred to the Duke of Normandy as *dux Northmannicae Britonicaeque regionis* and to his magnates as 'the counts and princes of the Normans and Bretons', even though he had to admit to a certain number of revolts.[16]

What is more surprising is that in the 1020s Dudo was already staking a Norman claim to the crown of England by relating how 'Alstelmus' (? Guthrum-Athelstan of East Anglia) gave Rollo half his kingdom in gratitude for his assistance in suppressing a rebellion.[17] True, Rollo is said to have given his share back to Alstelmus, but England still remained within Dudo's sights. He made one of Duke Richard's enemies incite the Frankish King to attack him by saying:

It is unworthy of your authority [*imperii*] that he [the Duke] has authority [*imperat*] over the Burgundians, reproves and threatens the Aquitanians, rules and governs the Bretons and Normans, threatens and devastates the Flemish, wins over and allies with the Danes, the Lotharingians and even the Saxons. The English also are obediently subject to him, and the Scots and Irish are ruled under his protection [*patrocinio reguntur*].[18]

Though this can only have been wishful thinking in the 1020s, it should be recalled that as early as 1002 Duke

Richard II had married his daughter Emma to King Ethelred the Unready, and that after Ethelred's defeat and death he obligingly provided a refuge for her sons, while she returned to England to marry her husband's victorious rival, Cnut, and so remain Queen of England till 1035. When one of the refugee sons, Edward the Confessor, eventually became King of England (1042), it could be seen as the result not so much of luck as of foresight, that he had spent twenty-five years of his life in Normandy, and that he was thought to have named his cousin, Duke William, as his successor and heir.

The difficulty about the conquests was that when they began to materialize, they could easily take the Normans away from Normandy and, so far as their connection with the land was concerned, denormanize them. The danger may not have seemed very great in the case of England, since the conquest was undertaken by the whole duchy, and both the Duke and his men retained their lands in Normandy in addition to their new acquisitions in England. The conquests made in Italy and Sicily, however, were different, since they were made by Normans who had emigrated from the homeland. Did the Normans in Normandy consider these conquests to be as Norman as their own conquest of England?.

It is well known that so far as Orderic Vitalis was concerned, the links between Italy and Normandy were very close. His own monastery of Saint-Evroul had been founded in 1050 by various members of the house of Giroïe who had, soon afterwards, been banished by the Duke and taken themselves off to Apulia. Even the Abbot, Robert of Grandmesnil, had had to go. Taking eleven monks with him, he had migrated to Italy and had eventually approached Robert Guiscard who had founded the abbey of Sant' Eufemia in Calabria for him. The Abbot's two half-sisters had followed, and one of them had married the Guiscard's brother, Roger the Great Count of Sicily. Another member of the family, William de Montreuil had, after a number of exploits, become commander of the papal army in Campania, where he was known as 'the good Norman'. His brother, Arnold of Echauffour, had had such a profitable time in Apulia that he had been able to return to Normandy and purchase the Duke's pardon, as a result of which the family of Giroie was in the quite exceptional position of being a noble family with lands in both countries. In addition Abbot Robert was able to revisit Normandy in 1077; and one of Arnold's sons, who became a monk at Saint-Evroul, visited Calabria twice, once staying for almost three years at Sant' Eufemia, where the liturgy was still chanted in the manner of Saint-Evroul, and where he may well have collected historical materials for Orderic.

Orderic's picture of these family and monastic connections is so vivid that there is a great temptation to assume that it was typical, and to generalize from it, but there are strong reasons for thinking that his experience was exceptional. Most Normans who went to Apulia won lands and (as Orderic put it) 'forgot Normandy';[19] they had emigrated because they had no land in Normandy, and consequently there was no reason for them to return. Very few of them belonged to noble families; in this respect, as in so many others, the Giroies were exceptional. No one knows the origin of Gilbert and Rainulf, the founders of the dynasty of Aversa-Capua – not even which part of Normandy they came from. And though it is well known that the sons of Tancred de Hauteville came from a place called Hauteville in the Cotentin, no one knows what happened to the Norman branch of the family. Unlike the Giroies, the Hautevilles made no monastic foundation to perpetuate their name in Normandy.

If we put Orderic on one side and examine the statements made about Italy and Sicily by other writers in Normandy, we find little evidence of any special or intimate knowledge. William of Jumièges (*c.* 1070–1) makes no mention of any Normans in those lands. The *Carmen de Hastingae Proelio* (?1067) has a baffling reference to 'Apulian and Calabrian, Sicilian whose darts fly in swarms'.[20] William of Poitiers (*c.* 1073–4) in his apostrophe to England refers to the fact that Norman knights 'possess Apulia, have conquered Sicily, are defending Constantinople and are making Babylon tremble', thus grouping the Norman adventurers in Italy and Sicily with those other Norman adventurers who sold their services to the Byzantine Empire.[21] But that is all.

The next generation of writers concentrated primarily on Robert Guiscard (d. 1085) and his son Bohemond, the incidents which attracted their attention being the victories over the Byzantine Emperor in Greece (1082–3), the Guiscard's success in forcing the Western Emperor, Henry IV, to retreat from Rome in 1084, and Bohemond's exploits on the First Crusade. Baudri de Bourgueuil in his *Carmen cxcvi* (*c.* 1099–1102) made William the Conqueror persuade his men to join in the English expedition by recalling their previous victories over the Mançeaux, the French, the Bretons, the Burgundians and the Angevins, adding that

Your [Norman] virtue also rules and restrains the laws of Apulia. The ferocity of Rome trembles at your names, hopes that our Guiscard will be as a thousand men, and grows feverish at the sound of his name.[22]

With this we are already in the land of legend, because the Guiscard's expedition to Rome did not take place until eighteen years after the conquest of England. But the general theme had been established. William of Malmesbury (*c.* 1125) was, as one might expect, less careless of chronology, but his only special contributions were the record of the Guiscard's epitaph (or four lines of it) at Venosa, and the story that William I 'used to stimulate and incite his own valour by recalling the memory of Robert Guiscard, and saying that it would be shameful to be outdone by him in feats of war, since in nobility he was his superior.'[23]

Towards the middle of the century this Guiscard material is caught up in what one can only describe as the saga of the Norman race. We can date the beginning of this development because Henry of Huntingdon, who had no such thing in his first edition of *c.* 1129, inserted two battle speeches in his edition of 1139, one of them attributed to Duke William at Hastings and the other to the Bishop of the Orkneys at the Battle of the Standard (1138), but which together form a complete statement of the theme. Slightly later (*c.* 1155–7) a very similar speech was written by Ailred of Rievaulx and attributed by him to Walter Espec at the same Battle of the Standard:

For why should we despair of victory, when victory has been given to our race, as if in fee, by the Almighty? Did not our ancestors [Rollo] invade a very large part of Gaul [Normandy] with a small force and erase the very name of Gaul from it with their people? How often did the Frankish army flee before them? How often did they snatch victory, even against great odds, from the men of Maine, Anjou or Aquitaine? And as for this island [Britain] which once upon a time the most glorious Julius won after a long time and after great slaughter of his men, for sure our fathers and we ourselves have conquered it in a short time, have imposed our laws upon it, and disposed of it at our will. We have seen – we have seen with our own eyes – the King of France and his whole army turn their backs upon us [at Mortemer, 1058], while all the best nobles of his kingdom were captured by us, some to be ransomed, others loaded with chains and others condemned to a dungeon. Who has conquered Apulia, Sicily and Calabria but your Norman? Have not both emperors [of the West and East] on the same day and at about the same hour, turned their backs on the Normans, though the one was fighting the father [Robert Guiscard at Rome in 1084] and the other his son [Bohemond in Greece in 1082]? Who, therefore, would not laugh rather than be afraid, when against men such as these, the vile Scot comes rushing into battle with his half-naked natives?[24]

At first sight this is the most magnificent example of Normanness, but seen in context it has strange features. The Scots had invaded England and were threatening York. In the resulting alarm the Archbishop had raised an army, by ordering all priests to lead their (English) parishioners with crosses, banners and saints' relics to an assembly-point where they would meet the (Norman) magnates. The army was then drawn up around a huge standard adorned with the banners of St Peter of York, St John of Beverley and St Wilfred of Ripon. The Archbishop was clearly calling for a holy war to defend the homeland, but Walter Espec said nothing of this. His speech was for Normans only. They were the professional warriors and the lordly class (the Norman myth did not entertain the possibility of a Norman peasant) and it was no doubt proper to address them, but they were not asked to defend their country (which country would it have been?), let alone to fight a holy war in its defence. Instead Walter's speech proclaimed a belief in Norman invincibility by reciting a catalogue of Norman victories from Rollo's conquest of Normandy in 911 to Robert Guiscard's march on Rome in 1084. In North Yorkshire in 1138 these might have sounded like tales of far away and long ago. There were no more Norman victories to cite; Henry I's great victory at Tinchebrai (1106) had been won with the help of the English against other Normans fighting for his brother, Duke Robert.

In examining the Norman myth we have commented on four main themes; the Frenchness of the Normans, their attachment to the land of Normandy, their Northman ancestry and their conquests or invincibility. In Walter Espec's speech there is no mention of the first two, presumably because they would not have been relevant in England. The speech concentrates solely on the Northman ancestry, which was supposed to make them invincible. But was their blood still that of the Northmen? Even if one was to assume that William the Conqueror was a 'pure' Norman, it would still be true that Stephen, who was king in 1138, was only Norman on his mother's side, and that three of his four grandparents were 'French' rather than Norman. And were they still invincible? In the next generations their confidence was to be shaken by a series of defeats culminating with the loss of Normandy itself (1204). If any Normans really thought that victory had been given to their race 'as if in fee by the Almighty', those final defeats must have helped them to realize that the victorious blood of Rollo was no longer pulsing in their veins. And when they realized that, there was nothing left of the myth at all.

33 Carving from the nave of Bayeux Cathedral (mid twelfth century); it was originally painted and was probably inspired by oriental silks, which were much coveted by wealthy Normans.

The Story of the Smith of Beauvais

(This story concerns Robert the Magnificent (1027–35), but it is only a story and is one of the interpolations made to William of Jumièges' history by a monk of Caen after 1087. It shows that at that date it was still realized that the dukes had encouraged immigration in order to build up a new nobility.)

Duke Robert was generous not only with words but also with gifts, and if he made anyone a gift in the morning he would keep on sending him everything that came to hand. One day a smith came from Beauvais and offered him two knives. The Duke told his chamberlains to give him 100 pounds Rouennais. The smith was just recovering from the shock when two nobles came from the Duke with two wonderful horses. At first the smith thought it was a joke or that he was just dreaming, but in the end he mounted one of the horses, and leading the other with his right hand, went home. Later in the evening the Duke sent further gifts, but then it was too late. 'But why', said the Duke, 'did he go so quickly, before he had been rewarded? Indeed if he had stayed a little I would have made him sit among the rich and noble.'

A year later, the smith returned to Normandy, bringing with him his two sons, well instructed in arms. He went to the Duke and said, 'Do you recognize me, your servant, O lord?' He said, 'No.' And the smith replied, 'I am he on whom you conferred magnificent presents last year, and I have come with my two sons to offer you faithful service, if Your Excellency will not refuse it.' (*Jumièges*, 106–8.)

Chapter Three

The Normans of the South: Italy and Sicily

The domination of the Normans in Italy and Sicily is one of the most romantic episodes in medieval history. Their conquest of the land in the eleventh century has all the best elements of a fairy story, since the Normans though few, and initially penniless, were able to win territories which were large, populous, rich and in a position of great strategic importance. They fought the emperors of East and West, played a large part in the affairs of the papacy (sometimes helpfully and sometimes not), and dominated the sea routes which were vital for the commerce of the Italian city-states. Culturally they also found themselves at the centre of things. In the twelfth century their kingdom was the meeting place of Latin, Greek and Arabic civilizations. Westerners who wanted to study Greek learning or to find translations of the works of Plato would find their way to Palermo where, in the king's court, they might also find the Arab geographer al-Edrisi whose great book, usually known, out of deference to the king, as *The Book of Roger* was illustrated by a map in the form of a planisphere which was said to have been of solid silver and to have weighed 450 Roman pounds.

Something of the intellectual excitement of the place is caught in the preface to the anonymous Latin translation of Ptolemy's *Almagest*. The writer says that he was studying medicine at Salerno (that in itself might have surprised a northerner) when he heard that a manuscript of the *Almagest* had been brought to Palermo by a man called Aristippus who had just returned from a royal embassy to

34 Monreale Cathedral, begun by King William II
in 1172, in an eclectic style of which the
dominant strains are Byzantine and Arabic.

Constantinople. He immediately sailed for Palermo, but found that he could not understand the book unless he improved both his Greek and his mathematics. Fortunately, however, he found a man called Eugenius who was expert in Latin, Greek, Arabic *and* mathematics, and with his help he made the translation. There was nowhere else in Europe where he could have had such luck. Eugenius, who, as his name implies, was of Greek origin, was one of the most famous men in the kingdom; he had already translated most of Ptolemy's *Optics* from Arabic into Latin, and as 'Admiral' (*ammiratus ammiratorum*, Emir of Emirs) he was to play an important part in the royal administration. Henry Aristippus, who brought the manuscript from Constantinople, was a Latin secular clerk who was to become Archdeacon of Catania; he was the translator of Plato's *Meno* and *Phaedo*, and was probably nicknamed Aristippus after Socrates' disciple of that name who spent so much time at Syracuse.

The reason for so much knowledge of Greek and Arabic was that while Apulia had been Byzantine, Sicily had been Moslem for the best part of two centuries. The Moslems were not ignorant of Greek philosophy – they had done much to preserve it – and in the Norman kingdom of Sicily they enjoyed a certain amount of toleration. We have an interesting description of the place by a Spanish Moslem called Ibn Jubayr who visited it – actually he was shipwrecked there – in 1184.[1] He was astonished at the number of Moslems in influential positions at the King's court. At Palermo they had their own suburbs with mosques and muezzins, and their own kadi to judge their lawsuits. At the King's court the pages were all (so he says) Moslem, and

35 Roger II portrayed in ecclesiastical vestments being crowned by Christ himself. Mosaic in the Martorana Church, Palermo.

if they find themselves in the presence of their master at the [Moslem] time of prayer, they go out of the King's chamber, one after the other, in order to recite their prayers – which they often do in some place within view of the King, but Allah (may he be exalted!) casts a veil over them.[1]

Once when there was an earthquake and the King saw all his concubines, handmaidens and pages praying to Allah, he was reputed to have said: 'Let each of you pray to the God he adores; he who has faith in his God will feel peace in his heart.' Yet this King, like his predecessors, apparently had the powers of a papal legate in Sicily and Calabria, and had himself portrayed in ecclesiastical vestments being crowned by Christ in person. When he died, he was buried like a Byzantine emperor with tiara, mantle and dalmatic in a sarcophagus of porphyry.

Like the Byzantine emperors also, the Norman kings had a state-owned silk factory, the earliest known product of which is the coronation mantle which was woven for Roger II in 1133–4 and which through his grandson, the Emperor-Frederick II, passed to the Holy Roman Emperors. It can still be seen at the Schatzkammer in Vienna. It is scarlet and gold, and portrays two tigers devouring camels, the design being so arranged that when the king wore the mantle, the eyes of the ferocious tigers would be glaring from in front of his shoulders. Round the rim is an Arabic inscription in Kufic lettering. In translation it reads:

[This mantle] belongs to the articles worked in the royal workshop, in which fortune and honour, prosperity and perfection, merit and distinction have their home. May the King rejoice in good acceptance, thriving magnificently in great generosity and high splendour, renown and magnificence and the fulfilment of wishes and hopes; may his days and nights be spent in enjoyment, without end or change; in the feeling of honour, dependency, and active participation in happiness and in the maintenance of well-being, support and suitable activity: in the capital of Sicily in the year 528 [of the Hedjira].[2]

The extraordinary ethos of the Norman Sicilian court can still be experienced at Palermo where many of its monuments have survived. The Capella Palatina or Palace Chapel has walls covered with Byzantine mosaics, a 'stalactite' or 'honeycomb' ceiling which is basically Arabic, and a magnificent ambo, or pulpit, decorated with carving and Roman Cosmati work. The King's private chamber in the palace has gold mosaics showing swans, peacocks, leopards, lions and centaurs displayed among ornamental trees as a pageant for an Oriental monarch. The church of the Martorana, founded in 1143 by the Admiral George of Antioch already in 1184 excited the wonder and amazement of Ibn Jubayr. Among its mosaics are portraits of both King Roger II and his Admiral, and (since the Admiral was a Syrian-Greek) a Byzantine hymn to the Virgin was inscribed in Arabic round the base of the dome. As for the cathedral of Monreale, it is basically a wooden-roofed basilica, but it looks cruciform and its walls are covered with an enormous expanse (8,000 square feet) of Byzantine mosaic, while outside the interlacing arches and circular medallions in polychrome suggest something more Arabic than Gothic, let alone 'Norman'.

English people who see these exotic buildings are normally amazed and ask in wonderment whether the Normans who built them were really 'our' Normans. In one sense they were, but in another they were not. And in order to explain why this was so it is necessary not only to say something about who they were, but also something about their lands and the way in which they gained possession of them.

75

36 *Above:* detail of the coronation mantle woven for Roger II in the
state-owned silk works at Palermo in 1133–4. It passed by inheritance to
the Holy Roman Emperors.

37 *Opposite:* mosaic from the King's private rooms in the palace at
Palermo: a pageant for an Oriental monarch.

38 Norman Italy and Sicily.

First the lands. These were quite a mixed bag, because at the beginning of the eleventh century, southern Italy and Sicily had no political or cultural unity. Politically there were three main groups of territories, first the three Lombard principalities of Benevento, Salerno and Capua, each one of which was in effect a separate state; secondly Apulia and Calabria, or the Byzantine 'catapanate of Italy', to which were attached the four little autonomous duchies of Amalfi, Sorrento, Naples and Gaëta; and thirdly the Moslem emirates of Sicily which were nominally dependent on the Zirids of North Africa.

These three political groups were also distinct culturally. The Lombard duchies were Latin in culture, Catholic in religion, and heavily influenced by the abbey of Monte

78

Cassino and the papacy. Apulia and Calabria were to a large extent Greek, supported the Greek Orthodox Church and had quite a flourishing Byzantine culture. Sicily, which had been ruled by Moslems for two centuries, had a large Arab or Berber population and a lively Arabic culture, but since it was not Christian, the Normans would be able to regard its conquest as a holy war.

The details of how the Normans first came to Italy are wrapped in obscurity. The one thing that is certain is that they did not come in a single body, but in small groups which were quite independent of each other and usually in bitter rivalry. They hired themselves out as mercenaries to various lords, changing masters whenever it suited them, often fighting against other Normans and sometimes moving on for a while to fight for, or against, the Byzantine Empire in Greece or Asia Minor. By playing their masters off against each other, some of the Norman mercenaries began to acquire land of their own and to emerge, first as minor, then as major, lords in their own right. By the 1060s they were beginning to form three rival blocs based on the previous political and cultural divisions of the country. In the Lombard principalities a Norman called Rainulf became Count of Aversa (1030), and in 1058 one of his successors was able to make himself Prince of Capua. Byzantine Apulia was the main preserve of the family of Hauteville; they captured Melfi in 1041, and in 1059 the most successful of them, Robert Guiscard (the Wily) was invested by the Pope as Duke of Apulia, Calabria and (if he could win it in the future) Sicily. In 1071 he captured Bari, the capital and last stronghold of the Byzantines in Italy, and in the following year he helped to capture Palermo, the capital of Sicily. But for all Robert Guiscard's theoretical claims, the real conqueror of Sicily was his younger brother Roger, who between 1060 and 1091 concentrated on this one objective.

39 Mosaic from the King's private rooms in the palace at Palermo.

40 George of Antioch, the 'admiral' or 'emir of emirs'. He is shown prostrate before the Virgin in a mosaic in the Martorana, the church he founded at Palermo in 1143.

41 This mosaic in Monreale Cathedral shows William II, robed more like a Byzantine emperor than a western king, offering the building to the Virgin.

42 Representation of Christ on
a coin of Roger II.

Because his was a holy war against the Moslems, Roger
had the wholehearted, unwavering support of the Church,
and his barons saw the war as a crusade against a single
enemy instead of (as on the mainland) a series of manœuvres
against a variety of different enemies, who could be played
off both against each other and against their rulers. As a
result, Roger was able to remain in undisputed control
of both the war and the government, and to dispose of
the conquered land at his will. Sicily, though the last of
the Norman bases to be established, was infinitely the
strongest, and it was a foregone conclusion that its ruler
would ultimately take control of all the Norman territories, as Roger II in fact did when he was crowned in
1130 as 'King of Sicily, the duchy of Apulia and the
principality of Capua'.

For the next half-century the wealth and culture of
Norman Sicily were at their apogee, attracting from abroad
the more recherché type of scholar in search of Greek
or Arabic science, and ambitious career-men, whether
clerical or lay. There were many vacancies for foreigners
in the Church, partly because the number of dioceses in
the kingdom was absurdly large – there were about 105

of them, 20 of them archbishoprics – and partly because a large proportion of the native population, being Greek or Moslem, was ineligible for ecclesiastical preferment. Laymen from abroad were likely to be rewarded with counties or lordships because the King, nervous of the rival factions within his kingdom, was always pleased to receive the service of foreigners who would be indebted to no one but him. English historians have fastened on the fact that some of these foreigners were English or Norman and have, wittingly or unwittingly, given the impression that they formed the great bulk of the immigrants. But this was not the case. The immigrants were cosmopolitan and included a large number of people from North Italy, Castile, Navarre and the non-Norman parts of France.

Though the Sicilian kingdom was splendid, it was never very stable. Internally it was divided, and externally it had no real friends. The Normans had won their position in Italy by playing off one ruler against another, and by attempting to control a precarious balance of power, both between rival states and between the empire and the papacy. Theoretically the whole of Italy belonged to the empire, which was German, and though in practice imperial power was normally confined to Northern Italy, the emperors made frequent attempts to extend it southwards to Rome, if only to try and control the pope. The papacy, therefore, was almost always in need of an alliance with the Normans. Realizing this, the Normans – both Robert Guiscard in the eleventh century and the Sicilian kings in the twelfth – sold their support dearly. Basically their interests coincided more nearly with those of the papacy than the empire, but if ever the pope seemed to be assuming their support too freely, the Normans would immediately raise their price by entering into negotiations with the emperor. They were very practised at this intricate form of diplomacy, but eventually

83

they overplayed their hand. In 1186 King William II, having no legitimate male heir, married his only daughter to Henry, the son of the Emperor Frederick Barbarossa. It was a disastrous mistake, because it divided the kingdom into two hostile camps, for and against the German alliance, and when William died (1189) there was civil war. Divided among themselves, the Normans could no longer control the balance of power, and after a couple of campaigns the Emperor Henry VI entered Palermo and was crowned King of Sicily (1194). The monarchy was no longer Norman but German.

43 Coin of Roger II (reverse).

44 *Opposite:* death of William II attended by his doctor, Ahmed, and an astrologer (*top left*); his funeral in the Capella Palatina (*top right*) to lamentations of the people of Palermo, counts, barons and court officials.

Though modern books refer to the 'Norman' kingdom of Sicily, the word 'Norman' did not figure in the King's titles. Nor did contemporaries, either within the kingdom or without, refer to it as 'Norman'. It was the 'kingdom of Sicily', and its king was the 'King of the Sicilians', the 'King of Sicily' or the 'Sicilian King'. The English chroniclers who recorded King Richard I's stormy visit to the island in 1190, on his way to the crusade, knew that the kingdom went back to the time of Robert Guiscard, but did not say anything to suggest that they considered

achim medic̄   rex w̄ eḡtꝰ   aſtroloḡ   plꝰt̃ eiꝰ   cappella Re
                                     Reg̃ defūcti   gia

porte panormi   coītes   et ßaronef   ðñi curie

it or its king to be Norman still. Like everyone else they thought of the Sicilians as being divided into three groups of peoples. There were the *Grifones* or Arabs (perhaps including some Greeks), the *Longobardi* or Latin-speaking natives, and the *ultramontanei* or *transalpini* who were the more recent arrivals from Northern Europe, such as the relatives and friends of Queen Margaret who arrived in the 1160s. It is important to realize that by the 1130s the great division was no longer between the Normans and the rest, but between those who (whatever their origin) had been born and bred in the kingdom and those who had just arrived.

The Sicilian kings showed not the slightest desire to appear Norman. Their ambitions were almost entirely Byzantine. They realized that their strategic position in Sicily gave them the opportunity to control the whole Mediterranean, and they looked forward to the day when they could conquer Byzantium and set themselves up as emperor. In many ways King Roger II behaved as if he were an emperor already. His Assises or laws were based on those of Justinian and endowed him with the absolutism of a Roman emperor, so that it was sacrilege even to dispute his judgments or question the worthiness of his officials. He enjoyed state monopolies (the silk industry, dye-works, stone-quarrying, iron-mining, salt, fisheries, forests and the manufacture of timber) and issued documents in the Byzantine style. Roger II's privilege for the abbey of La Cava was sealed with a golden bull, a prerogative really of the emperor, on which was engraved an inscription in Greek and an image of the King clothed in the manner of a Byzantine emperor.

On the mainland there had been a comparable assimilation in the eleventh century between the Normans and the Lombards. Most notable was the fact that Robert Guiscard found it desirable to divorce his Norman wife,

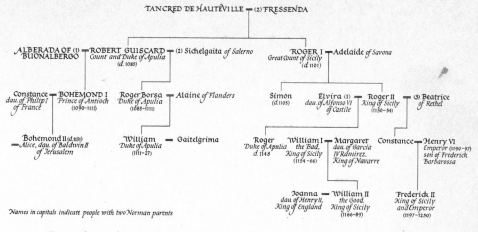

TANCRED DE HAUTEVILLE ⊤ (2) FRESSENDA

ALBERADA OF (1) ⊤ ROBERT GUISCARD ⊤ (2) Sichelgaita *of Salerno*   ROGER I ⊤ Adelaide *of Savona*
BUONALBERGO │ Count and Duke of Apulia │   Great Count of Sicily │
            │   (d. 1085)   │   (d 1101)

Constance ⊤ BOHEMOND I   Roger Borsa ⊤ Alaine *of Flanders*   Simon   Elvira (1) ⊤ Roger II ⊤ (3) Beatrice
dau. of Philip I │ Prince of Antioch   Duke of Apulia   (d.1105) dau. of Alfonso VI │ King of Sicily │ of Rethel
of France │   (1090-1111)   (1085-1111)   of Castile │   (1130-54)

Bohemond II (d.1131)   William = Gaitelgrima   Roger   William I ⊤ Margaret   Constance ⊤ Henry VI
= Alice, dau. of Baldwin II Duke of Apulia   Duke of Apulia the Bad, │ dau. of García   │ Emperor (1190-97)
of Jerusalem   (1111-27)   d. 1148   King of Sicily │ IV Ramirez,   │ son of Frederick
                                                         (1154-66) King of Navarre   Barbarossa

                                              Joanna = William II   Frederick II
                                              dau. of Henry II, the Good,   King of Sicily
                                              King of England King of Sicily   and Emperor
Names in capitals indicate people with two Norman parents   (1166-89)   (1197-1250)

45 Descendants of Tancred de Hauteville, the dominant dynasty of Italy and Sicily.

allegedly on grounds of consanguinity, in order to marry a Lombard princess, Sichelgaita of Salerno. According to William of Apulia this new marriage increased Robert's reputation and won him the willing obedience of the native population, which had previously obeyed him with reluctance.[3] It was doubtless for this reason also that Robert did not name as his heir the great warrior Bohemond who was the Norman son of his first marriage, but preferred Roger Borsa who, being the eldest son of the second marriage, had the blood of the Lombard princes of Salerno in his veins.

In spite of these facts the Normans in Normandy liked, as we have already seen, to boast of the Norman victories in Apulia, Sicily, Greece and Asia Minor as their own, and Orderic Vitalis succeeded in integrating them into his history. Is there anything to suggest that this feeling was reciprocated and that the Normans in the south were conscious of their Normanness and proud to be representatives of the Norman race? Or were the Normans of Normandy behaving rather like those nineteenth-century Englishmen who insisted that all Americans were really

87

British? To answer these questions we need to discover the myth of the Normans in Italy and Sicily, and as in the case of the Normans of Normandy, we start with a list of their most important contemporary historians.

Amatus of Monte Cassino, c. 1073–80. This, at any rate is thought to be the date of the lost Latin original, now known only from a fourteenth-century translation, *Ystoire de li Normant*, which has many obvious interpolations.

William of Apulia, c. 1095–9. *Gesta Roberti Wiscardi*.

Geoffrey Malaterra, soon after 1098. *De Rebus Gestis Rogerii Calabriae et Siciliae Comitis et Roberti Guiscardi Ducis fratris eius.*

Leo of Ostia (also known as Leo Marsicanus). *Chronicon Monasterii Casinensis*, begun in 1098 but revised both by himself and by Peter the Deacon in the first half of the twelfth century.

Alexander of Telese, c. 1140. *Rogerii Regis Siciliae Rerum Gestarum libri iv.*

Falco of Benevento, after 1154. *Chronicon de rebus aetatis sui.*

Romuald of Salerno, c. 1178–81. *Chronicon sive Annales.*

'Hugo Falcandus', after 1181. *Historia de Regno Siciliae.*

Peter of Eboli, c. 1195. *Carmen de Rebus Siculis.*

The first thing that strikes one about this list is how few of the works were written by Normans. In fact, none of them can be proved to have been by a Norman, though Geoffrey Malaterra is usually claimed as one because he states in his preface that 'coming from beyond the mountains' (i.e. the Alps), he had 'only recently become Apulian or indeed Sicilian' (*a transmontanis partibus venientem, noviter Apulum factum vel certe Siculum*).[4] The only other writer who could possibly have been a Norman is William of Apulia, though in his case a whole succession of learned editors and commentators have been unable to agree, and there remain strong arguments for his having been a native Apulian. Perhaps the difficulty in his case is that he did not regard the Normans as a strictly racial group.

In a famous passage he said that the Normans used to recruit all the brigands who sought refuge with them, 'teaching them their own language and customs so as to form them into one people'.[5] Language apart, this would accord well enough with what is known of the customs of the Northmen of Normandy, and reminds us of the fact that in Italy one of the earliest leaders of the Normans was a Lombard mercenary from Milan, called Ardoin.

A second observation, which may be a consequence of the lack of Norman authors, is that none of these historians attempted to see the activities of the Normans in the south as part of the wider achievements of the Norman race. Most of them concentrated on the careers of individuals such as Richard Prince of Capua, Robert Guiscard, or Roger the Great Count of Sicily. They stated quite bluntly that these men were Normans, but they considered them, not in a Norman context, but simply as part of the history of South Italy or Sicily. So far as they were concerned there was no question of what a modern historian has described as 'the manifold activities of the Normans . . . having everywhere formed part of a single endeavour'.[6] For them, Normandy was simply the land which their Normans had come from.

We can test the strength of their connection with Normandy by an examination of what they knew, or thought they knew, about the history of their great families before they migrated to Italy. The earliest such family was that of Aversa-Capua, the first recorded member of which in Italian history was a certain Rainulf, who was granted Aversa in 1130. What were his origins? According to Amatus (and at this point we can be reasonably certain of his text), the founder of the family was Gilbert Buatere (*Butericus*), a 'prince' or 'magnate' in Normandy who, in the course of a feud, killed another magnate called William Repostel, consequently incurred the anger of the Duke, who was Robert the Magnificent (1027–35), and fled to Italy with his four brothers, Rainulf, Ascletin, Osmund and Lofulde or Rudolf.[7] In Normandy Orderic recorded a similar story in his edition of William of Jumièges before 1109.[8] It may not be very important that he thought that the man who killed William Repostel was not Gilbert Buatere but Osmund Drengot, because Amatus and Leo both give Gilbert a brother called Osmund, but it is disconcerting to find him contradicting their statement that the family was noble. According to Amatus, Gilbert Buatere had been a 'prince' in Normandy, and Richard, son of Ascletin (the first of the family to become Prince of Capua), was his nephew. But Orderic did not think him noble at all. In his *Ecclesiastical History* he tells how Abbot Robert of Saint-Evroul, when exiled to Italy,

approached Richard Prince of Capua, son of Anquetil of the Quarrels [i.e. crossbow bolts), who gave him fair words but never followed them up with deeds. When Robert realized that he was being deceived by empty promises, he angrily reminded the prince of his base parentage, of which he was well aware.[9]

Obviously the princes of Capua preferred not to flaunt their low birth before the world, and if they wanted the world to think that their ancestors had been noble, they were prudent to be vague about the location of their Norman home. Since it has proved impossible to identify Gilbert Buatere, Osmund Drengot or even Anquetil of the Quarrels, it looks as if they succeeded in taking their secret to the grave.

About the house of Hauteville we seem at first to be better informed, perhaps because we have two early histories, by William of Apulia and Geoffrey Malaterra, which were written for, or dedicated to, members of the family. Malaterra specifically states that he got much of his information from the Great Count Roger. He tells us that the founder of the family, Tancred, possessed Hauteville in the Cotentin by hereditary right; that by his first wife, Muriel, he had five sons who were subsequently to become counts – William (Iron-Arm), Drogo, Humphrey, Geoffrey and Serlo; and that after the death of his first wife he married Fressenda, by whom he had seven more sons, Robert (Guiscard), Mauger, William (the second son of that name), Aubrey, Hubert, Tancred and Roger (the Great Count himself).[10] We are told that Fressenda was a good mother to her stepsons, but that they, seeing the difficulties which their neighbours had in providing a sufficiency for their sons, decided to leave Normandy and make their fortunes in Italy. One would assume that one son remained at home to enjoy the patrimony, and Malaterra tells us that it was Serlo, the youngest son by the first marriage, though three other sons (Mauger, Aubrey and Hubert) remained in Normandy also.

In order that such sons might not be considered of less worth than those who came to Italy, Malaterra thought it necessary to write something about Serlo, and promptly embarked on a variation of the story which Amatus had told about the Aversa family.[11] Serlo, he said, had been insulted by some magnate (*potente*), had killed him and, not being able to withstand the wrath of the Duke (Robert the Magnificent again), had fled to Brittany and from there had made raids across the Norman border. When Duke Robert was besieging *Teulerias* (? Tillières or Tilleul-en-Auge) Serlo heard that one of the French defenders was a Goliath-like man who kept challenging the Normans to single combat and killing them. So Serlo went there at break of day, challenged the man, defeated him, cut off his head, stuck it on his lance and paraded with it through the Duke's camp without saying a word. This heroic act earned him the Duke's pardon; his patrimony was restored, he was given a rich wife and was retained by the Duke among his *familiares*. One would have thought that William of Jumièges or Orderic Vitalis might have heard of him in Normandy, or that he would at least have been mentioned in a charter, but there is no trace of him. Orderic, who seems to have got his information at second hand from a garbled version of Malaterra, even thought that the name of the son who inherited was Geoffrey – though in this he was certainly wrong because Geoffrey was one of those who went to Italy.

Finally – and this is the actual order in which he gives the information – Malaterra tells a story about the original Tancred de Hauteville himself. Tancred, he says, was in the household of Duke Richard (996–1026). One day when the Duke was out hunting he started an enormous boar. The hounds pursued, but eventually the boar took up position with its back to a rock and turned on the hounds and rent them. Seeing this, Tancred plunged his sword through the beast's forehead, driving it in so deeply that only the pommel remained visible. Though it was against the rules for anyone to kill a beast which he had not himself started, the Duke was so impressed with the force of the sword-thrust, that he rewarded Tancred so that 'he served in the duke's court and had ten knights under him'.[12] Clearly we are supposed to see Tancred as a person of some consequence, but the Norman chronicles and records of the time carry no trace of him or of Hauteville. There are three Hautevilles in the Cotentin, and though antiquaries have turned one of the three into 'Hauteville-la-Guichard', there is no firm evidence for the identification.[13] The origin of the Hautevilles is hardly less mysterious than that of the Norman counts of Aversa, and one cannot help feeling that the family was content to leave it as vague and unsubstantiated as the dukes of Normandy left that of Rollo.

46 Norman knights: carving from the north doorway of
St Nicholas at Bari.

Some of the most vivid impressions derive from buildings,
and though those of Sicily are *sui generis*, there are some
on the mainland which seem at first sight to be Norman.
The most significant of these is probably the church of St
Nicholas at Bari, which is well known as the prototype
of Apulian Romanesque. Since Bari had till 1071 been the
capital of Byzantine Greece, it could well have been that
the Normans were determined to impress the inhabitants
with a large new church which was completely un-
Byzantine. That St Nicholas certainly is, but whether it
is Norman is a different matter. The wide west front with
its towers flanking, instead of masking, the side-aisles is
clearly Lombardic in inspiration, and though the internal
arrangement of arcade, triforium and clearstory could
have been derived from Normandy, it could also have
been derived from the great churches of Emilia – Modena,
Parma or Piacenza. As it happens, Orderic Vitalis tells us
that the person in charge of the building works was Abbot
Elias, who was not a Norman but an Italian and had
previously been a monk at La Cava near Naples.[14] In
church politics he was a high Gregorian, opposed to
Archbishop Ursus (d. 1089) who favoured the anti-pope
and was in touch with the Greeks, and it consequently
looks as if the church he built was intended to have an
ecclesiastical rather than a secular significance.

93

47 St Nicholas at Bari, west front. The building works were in charge of Abbot Elias, an Italian monk from La Cava.

94

Less beautiful but more dramatic is the cathedral at Aversa. Externally it is dull, mostly in an undistinguished Baroque of the eighteenth century, and internally the first impression is the same; it is cruciform with an aisled nave, central dome and aisleless chancel, all in the same heavy Baroque. But if one penetrates a small doorway in the transept, one finds oneself transported in place and time, for round the chancel, though now walled off from it, are the ambulatory and apsidal chapels of the Norman church. The ambulatory's quadripartite vaults with heavy ribs, and shafts with cushion-capitals are, if not Norman, at any rate North European, and it is only too easy to share Rivoira's enthusiasm and believe that this 'must' have been part of the church built by Richard, Prince of Capua in 1062, at a time when, as one might imagine, the Normans still thought and built in the manner of Normandy. Unfortunately this romantic idea has been disproved. Scattered remnants of Prince Richard's work have been identified and shown to be typical of the ordinary (non-Norman) work of eleventh-century Campania. The ambulatory and its radiating chapels must date from after the sack of the city by Roger II in 1135, and so far from being the work of Normans who were building in the only way they thought possible, must have been the result of a conscious effort to revive the memory of the Norman past.

Something very similar can be seen at the abbey of Venosa, the burial place of the early Hautevilles in Apulia. It has two churches. The earlier one, consecrated in 1059, is the one in which William Iron-Arm, Drogo, Robert Guiscard and his first wife, Alberada, were buried. It was originally an undistinguished building in the local style, re-using a certain amount of antique material and showing no trace of northern influence. The later church is quite different. Though never completed, it was planned on an

48 Aversa Cathedral: the heavy ribbed vaulting of   97
the ambulatory dates from after 1135 and may have
been a deliberate attempt to revive the memory of a
Norman past.

49 The mausoleum of
Bohemond at Canosa di Puglia,
reminiscent of a Moslem
turbeh.

50 *Opposite:* tomb of Roger II
in Palermo Cathedral. The
porphyry sarcophagus was the
colour of imperial purple.

imposing scale in the northern Romanesque style. Visitors
always like to imagine that this Romanesque church must
have been begun soon after 1063, when Robert Guiscard
reformed the abbey and appointed a Norman abbot,
Berengar, son of Arnold fitz Helgo (1063–94), who was a
former monk of Saint-Evroul. In fact it is much later,
dating from the third decade of the twelfth century.

It is all too easy to forget that because Robert Guiscard
left Normandy in 1046, he was never able to see any of
the great churches which we now call Norman, and that
even Abbot Berengar, who did not leave till 1061, could

not have seen more than the very earliest of them, Bernay, Mont-Saint-Michel and Jumièges, in course of construction. This is a fact which has to be remembered about almost all the Normans in Italy and in almost all spheres of life. They had left Normandy before the 'new Normandy' of William the Conqueror had taken shape, and consequently the Normandy they knew was very different from the Normandy we think of. Even in the twelfth century their knowledge remained hazy; the Romanesque church at Venosa is not in fact in the Norman style, but in the Burgundian.

It is interesting to compare the tombs or mausolea of the various members of the Hauteville family in Italy. Bohemond, the one wholly Norman son of Robert Guiscard, was buried at Canosa di Puglia in a mausoleum designed like a funerary *turbeh* outside a mosque, so as to recall his exploits on the first crusade and as Prince of Antioch. The two lengthy inscriptions recall his triumphs in Greece, Parthia, Syria and Antioch, but say not a word about his Norman ancestry. Roger the Great Count of Sicily was buried in an antique sarcophagus at the abbey of Mileto which has been destroyed by earthquake. His descendants, the Sicilian kings, were buried like emperors in massive porphyry sarcophagi amid the Byzantine glories of Palermo and Monreale. Robert Guiscard, Humphrey and Drogo, however, were all buried at Venosa. In the third decade of the twelfth century an attempt was made to commemorate the place with a grand Romanesque church which would recall their northern origin, but in the event it was left a half-built ruin. No one ever bothered to finish it. The King of Sicily was one of the richest monarchs in Europe and a Hauteville too, but he was too busy with his own projects to bother about his Norman past.

51 Columns in the cloister of Monreale Cathedral: the spiral polychrome inlay combines the Byzantine and Norman styles.

INCIPIT EPLA WILLMI CENOB
QVAS ORTODOXV AHALOR
LIHORAIAH HORVAI. DO

]O VICTORIOS
DO XO. SVM
anglor̄ regi
gēmeticensis cen
cenobicar̄ indi
willelm². ad co
stel sacrisonil, so
ad discernendū iu
abyssū O pus hoc
rex œ serenissime
ducū gestis de diue
codicibȝ iuxta mee
industrie contexui ur
celstudini. ob recolenda pscor̄ patru int pcis
dignitacū administrationes pississimor̄ actui
cronicor̄ bibliothere delegandū detreui. Quc
uenusta excornacū gūitate. ñ politi sermon
seu nicore. sed inelimato stilo. tenui oracione
tū culibet lectori ad liqdū elaboraui. vre q
lacera ambiunt pclari uiri litterar̄ picia a
q striccis gladiis ciuitatē circūeuntes. elumina
insidus. lectulū salomonis diuine legis puigil
latacunt tuem subtilissimi qqȝ ingenii uigi
pensatoris prerogatiua uobis collatū qliē u
mine. sic in cunctis qbȝ intendere. q ppende
ualere efficacia multa multimode pbaue
q tantilli nri laboris placida manu sum
gesta celebri memoria dignissima ur
phas paginas recolite Principiū nāqȝ na
ad Ricardū scdm a dudonis pici uiri histor
q posteris ppagandū karte comdauit. e
pui Ricardi fre diligent exsliuit. Reliq u
plurimor̄ ad corroborandā fide eque idoneor̄ a

Chapter Four

The conquest of England

The Norman conquest of England was a rare historical phenomenon. If the story were not so familiar, it would have been thought incredible that England, or any other country, could have been completely overwhelmed after a single battle. But that is what happened after the Battle of Hastings. Apparently as the result of one day's fighting (14 October 1066), England received a new royal dynasty, a new aristocracy, a virtually new Church, a new art, a new architecture and a new language. By 1086, when Domesday Book was made, less than half a dozen of the 180 greater landlords or tenants-in-chief were English. By 1090 only one of the sixteen English bishoprics was held by an Englishman, and six of those sees had been moved from their historic centres to large towns. By the end of the twelfth century almost every Anglo-Saxon cathedral and abbey had been pulled down and rebuilt in the Norman style. For almost two centuries the language of polite society – the aristocracy and the court – was French, and English was relegated to the underworld of the unprivileged.[1]

The effect of the Conquest on the people and institutions of England has been discussed by English historians in an almost endless succession of books and learned articles, and there is no need to rehearse their conclusions or their controversies again. What concerns us is not the effect of the Conquest on the English, but the effect which it had on the Normans themselves.

It hardly needs to be said that the Normans were extremely proud of their military achievement. The

52 *Opposite:* Orderic Vitalis's autograph copy of his edition of William of Jumièges. The illumination shows William of Jumièges presenting his *History of the Norman Dukes* to William the Conqueror.

53 Silver penny of King William I. It is in the traditional English style.

54 *Opposite:* a writ of King William I authorizing an exchange of land between two of his barons; note that it is addressed to 'baronibus suis fidelibus francis et anglis' – his faithful men French and English – with no mention of Normans.

Bayeux Tapestry is in large part a glorification of their military might. William of Jumièges in his history of the dukes took it as a matter of course that when it came to war, the Normans were superior to any of their neighbours, and William of Poitiers compared the Conqueror's English campaign with that of Julius Caesar, much to the disadvantage of the latter. Within historic memory there was no conquest comparable for its speed, completeness and permanence, unless perhaps a comparison of sorts could be drawn with Rollo's conquest of Normandy. The Normans could be excused for thinking that in war they had no peer.

A further stimulant to their pride was the fact that their Duke was now a king. In consequence he became the equal of the French king, and the Normans believed that thereby their status as a people was enhanced. There was admittedly the complication that though kings might be equal as kings, the French king was still the overlord of the Duke of Normandy; but the fact that their Duke was now a king encouraged the Normans to believe that his vassalage was not the same as the vassalage of other vassals. Henceforward when Normans referred to 'the king' in Normandy they no longer indicated the French king but their own king, and this, in combination with the fact that they were increasingly at war with the French,

prompted them to stress the fact that they were different. Dudo, it will be recalled, had tried to present the Normans as one sort of Frenchman, but now such comprehensive gallicization was no longer welcome; it was, as we have already seen, in the forty years after the Conquest that the terms *Normanni* and *Franci* ceased to be synonyms and came to be used in opposition to each other.

In one sense this was a curious result of the Conquest, because William's expeditionary force had not been wholly Norman. A sizeable number of his men, perhaps as many as a fifth or sixth of the whole, had been recruited from outside Normandy, notably from Brittany, Flanders, Artois and Picardy. Most notable of the Bretons were Alan of Richmond and his brother Brian, Judhael of Totnes, Wihenoc of Monmouth, Alfred of Lincoln, and Oger the Breton of Bourne; and of the Flemings or near-Flemings, Eustace of Boulogne, Gilbert of Ghent, and Arnulf of Hesdin. It was perhaps because of the diverse origins of these men that the writs which William issued in England were always addressed to his faithful men '*French* and English'. But since the invasion had been organized by, and for the benefit of, the Duke of Normandy, the colloquial usage was to call all his followers 'Normans', and by the twelfth century this had become the general rule. By 1125 William of Malmesbury automatically divided the inhabitants of England into Normans and English, and it has only been after much detailed research that modern scholars have been able to establish which of these so-called Normans were not Norman at all.

At first sight it might have been thought that many difficulties would have been created by an army of such mixed origins. The Bretons were notorious for their wars or 'rebellions' against the Normans, and it might have seemed a real danger that in England they would disobey the Duke or quarrel with his Norman followers. In Normandy it was difficult enough to keep the Norman barons in order without adding the complication of Bretons, Flemings or Frenchmen who were not in the habit of obeying any superior at all.

Fortunately for the Conqueror, the circumstances of the Conquest militated against such divisions. Whatever a baron might normally think of rebelling against his lord, rebellion in England was bound to be seen as something very much more serious. All William's followers had been rewarded with lands in England, and all could lose them in the twinkling of an eye if they fell out among themselves and provided the opportunity for a rising of the English. Therefore, though homage and fealty were already serious matters in any part of North-West Europe, in England they were more serious still, being, so far as the Normans were concerned, the only means of survival. In France or even Normandy there was always a danger that the king or duke would be unable to muster a large enough army against rebels because some of his barons might be in secret sympathy with them. In England in the years immediately after 1066 such secret sympathies were rare, because all William's men knew that one successful rebellion could imperil their whole dominion.

55 Two aspects of feudalism in Normandy before 1066. William the Conqueror (*left*) receives the keys of the castle of Dinant from Conan Count of Brittany and (*right*) invests Harold, his future rival in England, with arms, thus making him in some sense his vassal or 'man'.

The Conquest, therefore, provided both an opportunity and a need to strengthen the feudal institutions which bound the Normans together. Before 1066 feudalism was more developed in Normandy than in England, knight-service already being a recognized institution with many feudal quotas already fixed, but in the process of the Conquest not only was the Norman model introduced into England, but it was made far more effective and systematic than it had ever been in Normandy. This was because, as Conqueror, William claimed the whole of England as his, every inch of it. He dispossessed all but a handful of English lords and gave their lands to his own men to be held of him by feudal tenure, insisting that he, the King, was the only person who was allowed to regard land as his absolute and inalienable property. Everyone else was merely a tenant and paid rent, normally in the form of knight-service. Even in the case of the English bishoprics and abbeys, William allowed them to retain their lands only on condition that they became his tenants and rendered knight-service.

56–7 The speed and efficiency with which the
Normans erected castles was decisive for the
conquest of England. *Above:* a *motte* or earthen
mound being constructed round a wooden
tower at Hastings. *Right:* one of the two *mottes*
erected at York in 1068–9 on opposite sides of
the Ouse. The tower on top, 'Clifford's Tower',
dates from the thirteenth century.

He was thus able to establish for himself a position which other kings might have dreamt of, but which had never existed before, either in Normandy or in any other part of Europe. He was both king and feudal lord of absolutely all the land in his kingdom – the sole fount of justice and the sole source of wealth. England thus became the first and most perfect example of a feudal monarchy, the New Leviathan of the medieval world. The Normans, apart from William himself, probably did not like it; for them it must have seemed as if the King held them bound hand and foot. He could give them land, but he could (and often did) take it away. Thanks to the efficiency of the Old English administration, he was able to compile, in Domesday Book, a survey of all his landed property in England (i.e. of the whole kingdom), so that he could ascertain that none of his men had seized lands which he had not granted them, and so that he could determine how much to charge sons for the privilege of being granted the lands of their fathers.

A similarly ruthless systematization can be seen in the construction of castles. Before 1066 castles were almost non-existent in England – we know only of five, all built by Edward the Confessor's Norman or French favourites – and Orderic Vitalis stated bluntly that it was the lack of castles which was one of the main reasons for the English defeat. The Normans, on the other hand, were well used to castles – we know of at least forty which were erected in Normandy before 1066 – and they were quick to see that if they were to hold the conquered country, they would have to build castles in very large numbers, and speedily.

There has been a certain amount of controversy about these castles in recent years.[2] It used to be thought that there was a standard pattern of castle in Normandy for twenty or thirty years before 1066, and that this consisted of an enclosure (bailey) with a wooden tower on top of an enormous mound called a *motte*. It now seems clear that this pattern was far from being general in pre-Conquest Normandy; and that though *mottes* were known, they were rare. Their emergence as the regular and inevitable feature of a Norman castle was due to the conquest of England. What was needed in England was a form of castle which could be defended by a small number of Normans against a large number of English, and yet could be constructed with speed. For these purposes the *motte* was ideal. In constructional terms it consisted of a tall wooden tower with a large mound of earth heaped round its base so as to protect it from incendiaries. Wood and earth were materials which, unlike stone, could be found almost anywhere, so that there would be no problem of finding quarries or masons, let alone of arranging for the transport of the stone. All that was needed was a large number of men to pile up the earth, and in England this was easy because the Normans could command an endless supply of forced labour. The consequent speed of erection is suggested by the Bayeux Tapestry, which shows the construction of a *motte* at Hastings, although the army was only there for fifteen days. Similarly Orderic Vitalis says that in 1068, in the course of punitive expeditions, the Conqueror built castles at Exeter, Warwick, Nottingham, York, Lincoln, Huntingdon and Cambridge, and all of these except Exeter (which was in an angle of the Roman wall) and Nottingham (which was a cliff-top site) were *mottes*.[3] When there was more time, or more splendour was required, something more elaborate could be attempted, but this, as in the case of the Tower of London or Keep at Colchester, would probably not have been till the 1080s or 1090s, after the military urgency was passed. Until then, *mottes* were standard equipment.

58–9 It was only gradually that stone towers were built to replace wooden ones in castles. Though there was some sort of stone castle at Rochester from *c.* 1088, the present Keep (*below*) dates from *c.* 1126. St George's Tower at Oxford Castle (*opposite*) is much earlier, probably *c.* 1074. It is not on the *motte* but on the edge of the bailey, adjoining the chapel of St George for which it may also have served as a bell-tower.

Once they had settled down, the Normans found that they were enormously wealthy. England was four or five times larger than Normandy and, thanks to its wool trade, a good deal richer. Most Normans received far larger estates than they had in Normandy. The two brothers Ilbert and Walter de Lacy, who held between them eight estates of some size in Normandy, received in England lands reckoned at an annual value of £251 (for Ilbert) and £397 (for Walter), and this at a time when a 'normal' knight's fief cannot have been worth more than about £20 a year. Roger Bigod, who may not have held more than half a knight's fief in Normandy, received in England lands to the value of about £500 a year, while Odo, Bishop of Bayeux benefited to the tune of about £1,750 a year. King William himself retained lands worth £12,500 a year, but this was by no means the whole of his revenue. In addition there were the enormous feudal 'incidents' which he could demand from his tenants, and the Old English taxes (especially the land tax called *geld*) which had made the Anglo-Saxon kingdom about the richest in Europe.

The Normans soon displayed their riches in the splendour of new buildings which were designed to be bigger and better than anything which had gone before. In England we are now so accustomed to the sight of Norman architecture that we often forget the extent of the achievement in material terms. The number of major churches rebuilt in whole or in part before 1100 is staggering; they include the cathedrals of Canterbury, Lincoln, Old Sarum, Rochester, Winchester, London, Chichester, Durham and Norwich, and major abbey churches at Battle, St Augustine's Canterbury, St Albans, Bury St Edmunds, Ely, Gloucester, Tewkesbury, Chester and St Mary's York. They were all large and several of them were among the largest in Europe. In the following century, in addition

114

60 In spite of much rebuilding, St Albans Abbey still preserves some impressive Norman architecture of the eleventh century, including the central tower which dates from the 1080s or 1090s.

to a further number of major churches (Peterborough, for example), parish churches were built or rebuilt in almost every town and village. Clearly such a vast amount of work could not have been executed unless there was already a flourishing building industry in England, but although the workmen (both skilled and unskilled) were probably English, the design of the new churches was peculiarly Norman and, as in the case of the castles, almost more so than in Normandy.

115

61 The East Anglian see was moved from Thetford to Norwich in 1094,
and the present cathedral was begun in 1096. The south nave aisle (*opposite*)
probably dates from the 1120s.

62 Bronze sanctuary knocker, Durham Cathedral. The beast's head
originally had enamelled or glazed eyes.

63–5 *Left:* Castle Acre Priory, Norfolk; part of the west front (*c.* 1150) with its interlacing arches. *Above:* the enormous scale of the Normans' buildings is shown in the way that cathedral and castle dominate the town at Durham. *Right:* Gloucester Abbey (now the cathedral); Gothic vaulting on the Norman nave.

118

It comes as something of a surprise to find how small was the number of major churches built or rebuilt in Normandy before 1066. Some, like the cathedrals of Rouen and Coutances, have subsequently been rebuilt again, but even allowing for such losses the number is small. In those that are still standing – the abbey church at Bernay (*c*. 1017–50), the naves of Mont-Saint-Michel (*c*. 1040) and Jumièges (*c*. 1042–67) and the chancel of the Abbaye-aux-Dames at Caen. (1062) – one can see quite clearly the origin of the Norman style, but with the exception of Jumièges they do little to prepare one for the grandeur, lavishness and daring of those that were erected after the Conquest. It was at Durham, soon after 1093, that was solved the central problem of medieval architecture, how to erect, and keep up, a stone roof over the highest parts of a church without making it impossible to have any windows or other openings in the walls; the vital combination was a groined vault with ribs and pointed transverse arches. Some historians have thought it strange, and even incredible, that this engineering feat should have been first accomplished in the northernmost outpost of England rather than the more sophisticated parts of Italy or France, but the truth of the matter was that no one but a Norman in England could have been rich enough to experiment on such a gigantic scale. Winchester Cathedral had no such remarkable vault, but was probably the longest in Europe; its central tower collapsed in 1107 but, money being no object, it was rebuilt immediately. At Westminster palace the King's new hall, completed in 1097, was for more than a century by far the largest in Western Europe. Measuring 238 feet by 68 feet, it was more than double the size of the emperor's hall at Goslar, but the story got around that when William Rufus saw it, he said it was 'not big enough by half'.[4]

66 Westminster Hall. The lower walls are those of William II's building of 1097, which he thought 'not big enough by half'.

It was not only unlimited riches which enabled the Normans to erect their most typical buildings in England. Another reason was that in England they were unrestrained by the past. For political reasons they were often glad to sweep away Anglo-Saxon buildings which might have historical associations of a dangerous kind, and they doubtless found it desirable to make their buildings much larger than the old, so as to impress on the English that their new masters were supermen. Even the audacity of their feats of engineering may have been a form of propaganda or boasting, to demonstrate that the Normans could do what others thought impossible.

★

The paradox of the Normans is that though it was in England that they reached their acme and fulfilled themselves as Normans, yet in the long run the conquest of England turned them into Englishmen. The first sign of what was to come could be seen in the Conqueror's new title; he was King not of the Normans but of the English. Historians have often explained how advantageous, and even necessary, it was for William to take this title and appear as the lawful successor of Edward the Confessor, but they have usually added that he and his successors revealed their essential Normanness by spending about as much time in Normandy as in England. That, however, is to put the cart before the horse, because the real point to explain is why the Normans spent as *much* as half their time in England. It was not just the king but also his nobles. Though they retained their Norman lands and Norman names (de Bohun, de Mandeville and the like), their Norman homes cannot have seen very much of them.

For this the most obvious reason was probably money. As we have already seen, the Normans, both individually and collectively, were richer in England than in Normandy. But their money did not come like dividends through the post; it had to be collected from a reluctant people. Both king and nobles had to be for ever on the watch to see that officials collected their demesne revenues in full, enforced the feudal incidents in full, and (particularly before the completion of the Domesday survey) allowed no rival Norman to 'invade' their land. At a time when the lordship of almost all the secular land in England had changed, it would have been easy for individuals to profit from the general confusion and claim, or seize, particular lands, revenues or rights which had really been granted to someone else. Even the king could not assume that his sheriffs would not embezzle his property, and all the Normans, high or low, had to accept that if they did not wish to lose the rights they had been given, they would have to keep a watchful eye on them.

After the death of William I the various succession wars encouraged a division between those who lived primarily in England, and those who lived primarily in Normandy. All Normans would have agreed that such a division was undesirable, but conditions were such that they sometimes had to accept it as the least of evils. When the Conqueror's eldest son, Robert, was Duke of Normandy but in dispute with his two younger brothers, who were successive Kings of England, it was very difficult for the nobility to maintain friendly relations with both sides. In Normandy Robert tended to be easy-going, but in England William II and Henry I ruthlessly dispossessed those who supported him, and systematically distributed the forfeited estates among 'new men' who had little or no land in Normandy and consequently stayed in England more permanently.

Once England had become the principal residence of most Normans, it was inevitable that they would intermarry with the English; and though we know very few of the details, it is certain that they did. Near the bottom end of the social scale the leading chroniclers of Normandy and England, Orderic Vitalis (1075–1141) and William of Malmesbury (c. 1090/6–1143) were both half English. At the very top, Henry I married the great-granddaughter of Edmund Ironside within little more than three months of his accession (1100). The fact that she changed her name from Edith to Matilda is an example of the difficulty which genealogists have in proving identities at this period, but it is probably true that soon after the Conquest Robert d'Oilli, the first castellan of Oxford, married the daughter of Wigod of Wallingford, and it is certain that Simon de Senlis I married the daughter of Earl Waltheof. By the 1180s intermarriage was so general that, according to the Dialogue of the Exchequer

Nowadays, when English and Normans live close together and marry and give in marriage to each other, the nations [*nationes*] are so mixed that it can scarcely be decided (I mean in the case of the freemen) who is of English birth and who of Norman.[5]

It may be thought strange that this development occurred during the middle years of the twelfth century, because it was exactly during that period, both in England and in Normandy, that the Norman myth was at its height. As we have already seen, Henry of Huntingdon had no normanizing battle speeches in his first edition of 1129, but added them, complete with references to Rollo, in his edition of 1139. Walter Espec's battle speech, said to have been delivered in 1138, was written up by Ailred of Rievaulx in the 1150s. Wace's *Roman de Rou* dates from c. 1160–74, and Benoît de Sainte-Maure's *Chronique des Ducs de Normandie* from 1172 to 1176. The more French the Normans were becoming in Normandy, and the more English in England, the more they insisted on their Danishry and their descent from Rollo.

67 A page of Domesday Book with entries relating to the royal demesne in Hampshire and the Isle of Wight. The regular formula is 'ten(et) rex' or 'ten(et) rex in d(omi)nio'.

IACOBE. Lang tenuit de rege .E. T.R.E. se defd p xiii. hid.
xii. tra .e. xii. car. In dnio te .ii. car. 7 iiii. serui. 7 xxi. uitti.
xi car. Ibi molin de .xx. solid. 7 xiiii. ac pa. 7 pascua .Li. den.

Rex ten in dnio SVDBVRNE IN SVDBVRNE hund.
Regale m fuit. sed n fuit p hidis distribut. Tra .e.
x. car. In dnio sunt .ii. car. 7 xx.v. uitti. 7 iiii. bord
cu eis. Ibi .ii. serui. 7 ii. molin de .xv. solid. Ibi
vii. colibi 7 xx. ac pa. pascua de xvii. sot. 7 x. denar.
de herbag. huic ptin soca duor hund. Ibi .ii. eede
quib ptin dim hida in elemosina.

Prefec callumn ad op hui m una v tre 7 pascua qua
uocat duna. que redd .xv. solid. Comes morton tenet.
Sed hund testat q in dnica firma regis iacere debet.
Ibi funt .T.R.E. 7 pai in eos.

HE TERRE INFRA SCRIPTE IACENT IN INSVLA DE WIT.

Rex ten in dnio CHENISTONE 7 DONE. Oda ibi hoes tenuer
in alodiu de rege .E. Te geldau p .ii. hid. modo p nichilo.
Oda cu .ii. tbis hoib, habuit dimid hid. 7 quarta parte
uni v. Aluuold .i. uirg. herolds .i. uirg. Goduin .i. uirg.
Alric una v. Brictric dim hid. Vnquisq, hor parte
molin. quep, parf. xxii. denar. hor v. car 7 hoi qra
ten rex in firma sua. T.R.E. ibi .ii. car in dnio. 7 appetiit
c. sot. 7 tam redd .viii. lib de firma.   .v. solid.

R de Oda tenuit .xii. sot. R de Aluuold .v. sot. R de herold.
LADONE 7 BEDINGEBORNE ten rex in dnio. Oda
tenuit in alodiu de rege .E. Te geldau p .iiii. hid. 7 m
p dim hida. Tra .e. iiii. car. Rex ten in firma sua. Oda
habeb .iiii. lib. de firma.

SANDFORD CV WICA ten rex in dnio. Rex .E. tenuit.
Te .iii. hide. X do uicecom recep .ii. hide 7 una v.
Tra .e. xii. car. In dnio sunt .iii. car. 7 x. uitti 7 iiii. bord
cu vi. car. Ibi .x. serui. 7 ii. molin de .Lxx. denar.
7 vi. ac pa. De herbagio .xx. sot. Silua sine pasnagio.
T.R.E. xx.v. lib ad pensu 7 ursura. X do rex recep .xx.
lib. simili modo. 7 ne m xx. lib ad pensu 7 redd de
firma .xx.vii. lib ad pensu. 7 c. denar.

ADRINTONE ten rex in dnio. Rex .E. tenuit. Ibi .iiii. hide.
Tra .e. v. car. In dnio sunt .ii. car. 7 x. uitti 7 xii. bord
cu .x. car. Ibi vii. serui. un molin de .xv. solid.
hui m ecctam ten abb de lira. cu una v tre. un ac
pa. 7 oim decima m. 7 appetiat .xx. solid.
Totu m T.R.E. ualb .x. lib. 7 post 7 m. viii. lib. Tam
redd .xii. lib. blancas. de .xx. in ora.

EVERELANT ten rex in dnio. Rex .E. tenuit. Non fuit
hidat. Tra .e. v. car. Ibi sunt .xii. uitti cu .v. car.
T.R.E. ualb .c. sot. 7 post 7 m. Tam redd .c. solid.

ABEDESTONE ten rex in dnio. Tres ibi hoes tenuer
in alodiu de rege .E. Te m geldau. p una hida. Tra .e.
ii. car. Hi sunt m cu .ii. uitti 7 v. car. Val 7 ualu. xl.
solid. Tam redd .Lx. sot. alias.
In insula hr rex un frustu tre. unde exeut .vi. uomeres.

SCALDEFORD ten rex in dnio. S.uuord tenuit in alodiu

de rege .E. Te m geldau p dim hida. Tra .e. i. car. Ibi sunt .iii. uitti
teu car. 7 dim. Val 7 ualu. xiii. sot. Tam redd .xvi. sot. 7 iiii. deri.

LISCELANDE ten rex in dnio. Quinq, libi hoes tenuer in alodiu
p .v. maner de rege .E. Te geldau p una hida 7 dimidia uirga.
Modo p dim hida 7 dim uirga. Almar habuit dim hida. Vlnod
dim uirg. Suaran dimid v. Odeman. dim v. Godman. una v.
Tra .e. ii. car. Ibi sunt .iiii. hoes in dnio. car 7 dim. 7 v. ac
pa. Val 7 ualut. xx. solid.

IOVECVBE ten rex. Sauuin tenuit in alodiu de rege .E. Te
geldau p una hida. m p .ii. parab. uni v. Tra .e. i. car. 7 ibi .e.
in dnio. cu .vi. bord 7 ii. serui. T.R.E. ualb .iiii. lib. 7 post 7 m.
iii. lib. Tam redd de firma. iiii. lib.

NONOELLE ten rex. Visflet tenuit de rofa. sed n fuit alodiu. Te
geldau p .ii. hid. modo p una v. Tra .e. i. car 7 dim. In dnio .e. car
7 i. uitti 7 ii. bord cu dim car. 7 ii. serui. T.R.E. ualb .ix. sot. 7 post
7 modo. xl. sot. 7 tam redd de firma alba.

LACHERNE ten rex. herald tenuit. Te geldau p una hida. m pro
nichilo. Tra .e. i. car. 7 ibi .e. in dnio. cu .ii. bord 7 v. serui.
T.R.E. ualb .xxv. solid. 7 post 7 modo. xx. solid.

VLWARTONE ten rex. Edd eus tenuit de Goduino. Te geldau p di
mia hida. m p nichilo. Tra .e. i. car. 7 ibi .e. in dnio. cu .iiii. bord
7 uno seruo. Val 7 ualut. x. sot.

SANDE ten rex. Vlnod tenuit de rege .E. in alodiu. Te geldau
p .ii. hid. modo p dimid 7 dim v. Tra .e. iii. car. In dnio .e. una car.
7 ii. uitti 7 uno bord. cu .ii. car. 7 ii. ac pa. Valut. xl. sot. m xxx.

WAROCHESSELTE ten rex. Gueda comitissa tenuit de Goduino
in alodiu. Te geldau p .v. hid. Modo p .ii. hid 7 dimid. Tra .e. x. car.
In dnio sunt .iiii. car. 7 x. uitti 7 xiiii. bord cu .vii. car. Ibi .xiii.
serui. 7 ii. molin de .xx. solid. 7 iii. ac pa. Silua de uno porc.
T.R.E. ualb .xx.vii. lib. 7 post 7 m. xx. lib. Tam redd .xvi. lib.

HASELIE ten rex. herald tenuit. Te geldau p .iii. hid. modo
p una v 7 dim. Tra .e. iii. car. In dnio sunt .i. 7 iiii. uitti 7 iiii. bord
cu .ii. car. Ibi .xx. serui. 7 x. ac pa. Silua de .ii. porc. [de xx. m pa]
T.R.E. ualb .viii. lib. 7 post 7 m. c. sot. Tam redd .viii. lib de firma.

BENVERESLEI ten rex. Goduin tenuit de rege .E. in alodiu. Te geldau
p una hida. m p dim hida 7 dim v. Tra .e. ii. car. Ibi .e. una uitti
cu una car. Silua. de uno porc. Valut. xl. sot. m. xx. solid.

CHOCHEPON 7 BILARDEN ten rex. Duo libi hoes tenuer p .ii.
maner in alodiu de rege .E. Te geldau p una hida. m p .iii. uirg.
Tra .e. i. car. 7 ibi .e. cu .iii. uitti. Valuit. xxx. sot. Modo. xx. sot.

HOTELESTON ten rex. Vlnoc tenuit   Tam redd .xxx. sot.
de rege .E. in alodiu. Te geldau p tcia parte hide. modo p dim
uirg. Tra .e. dim car. 7 ibi .e. cu .iii. bord. Valut. x. sot. n. .v. sot.

STANEBERLE 7 WIPISSEHA ten rex. Cheping tenuit in
alodiu de rege .E. p .ii. maner. Te geldau p .ii. hid. m p .ii. hid.
Tra .e. vii. car. In dnio sunt .ii. 7 vii. uitti 7 x. bord. cu .iii. car.
Ibi .xii. serui. 7 v. ac pa. Val 7 ualut sep .xii. lib.

WENECHETONE ten rex. Duo libi hoes tenuer in alodiu de
rege .E. p duob m. Te geldau p una hida. m p nichilo. Tra .e.
ii. car. 7 ibi sunt cu .ii. uitti. Valut 7 ualt. lii. lib.
De his tam duob m exeut de firma .xviii. lib. de .xx. in ora.

68 The best manuscript of Gaimar's History of the English. Though it was
written in French it helped the Normans to become English.

It often happens that the most elaborate statements of
a belief are made at a time when its adherents know that
it is seriously threatened, and are consciously trying to
bolster it up, and this may well be the explanation of the
normanizing literature of the third quarter of the twelfth
century. To judge from the very small number of manu-
scripts that have survived, it would seem that the circula-
tion of the *Roman de Rou* and *Chronique des Ducs de
Normandie* was small.[6] So far as popular appeal was concerned they were outshone by the counter-myth which
can be seen emerging at this same time.

This counter-myth is most obvious in the History of the
English (*L'Estoire des Engleis*) which was written by Geffrei
Gaimar (c. 1135–40). Like Wace and Benoît, Gaimar wrote
in French, but unlike them he lived in England, probably

in Lincolnshire or East Yorkshire; and whereas Wace and Benoît tell the stories of the Normans from Rollo to King Henry I, Gaimar tells that of the English from Hengist to the same King Henry I. But the most remarkable feature of his work is the treatment of the Norman Conquest, which he somehow manages both to describe and to pass over with studied casualness. He has an account of the Battle of Hastings but it is brief and concentrates on the picturesque story of Taillefer so as to exclude most of the fighting. He says hardly a word about Harold, and (perhaps in consequence) manages not to take sides between Normans and English; he succeeds in telling even the story of Hereward without creating an anti-Norman (or anti-English) atmosphere. He gives no impression of the Norman Conquest being a conquest, the only domination of the English about which he writes with bitterness being that of the Danes. On the death of Harthacnut:

> Great joy the English made.
> For the Danes held them cheap,
> Oftentimes they shamed them.
> If a hundred met one alone,
> It was bad for them if they did not bow to him.
> And if they came upon a bridge,
> They waited; it was ill if they moved
> Before the Dane had passed.
> In passing each made obeisance,
> Who did it not, if he was taken,
> Shamefully men beat him.
> So cheap were the English.
> So the Danes insulted them.[7]

Gaimar tells us a good deal about the sources he had used for his history. They did not include any from Normandy. The most important were the Anglo-Saxon Chronicle, which he calls 'the book of Winchester' and from which he got his basic facts, and Geoffrey of Monmouth's *Historia Regum Britanniae,* which he called 'the books of the Welsh about the British kings'. Geoffrey of Monmouth was one of those Normans who was really a Breton, and it is hard to say how much of his fanciful Arthurian history was Breton folklore, Welsh folklore or pure invention, but it seems clear that one section of his book, the prophecies of Merlin, provided Gaimar with his basic theme. These prophecies (according to Geoffrey of Monmouth) were made as an interpretation of Vortigern's dream about a battle between a red dragon and a white dragon. That battle signified (said Merlin) the struggle between the Britons (red) and the Saxons (white), and it would only be ended when there should come 'a people dressed in wood and in iron corselets' who would 'give their dwellings back to the earlier inhabitants' (i.e. the British). Geoffrey of Monmouth clearly intended this new people to be seen as the Normans in their ships and their coats of mail, and Gaimar followed him. But, as was perhaps natural for someone in Lincolnshire and East Yorkshire, he did not accept the dragons as the British and the English, but treated them as the English and the Danes, explaining that Ethelred the Unready's marriage to Emma of Normandy was a deliberate bid by the English for an alliance with the Normans against the Danes:

> If the Normans are his friends
> He could easily subdue his enemies.[8]

It is both interesting and important to see how Gaimar came into possession of Geoffrey of Monmouth's history. He says that his patron, the Lady Constance, got her husband, Ralph fitz Gilbert, to borrow it from Walter Espec of Helmsley (he of the normanizing battle speech). Walter had been sent it by Robert Earl of Gloucester (d. 1147) who had had it translated from the Welsh.[9] It is a most interesting example of the immediate and enormous success of Geoffrey of Monmouth's book, but it also emphasizes the importance of Robert Earl of Gloucester, for whom it was written and to whom it had originally been dedicated (*c.* 1135). Earl Robert, who was an illegitimate son of King Henry I, held one of the largest honours in England and Normandy. He had very large estates in the west of England, and was also prominent in Wales as Lord of Glamorgan. In Wales he would doubtless have found it useful to be well versed in Arthurian history and to encourage the Welsh to believe that he was their natural ally against their old enemies the English.

In England, of course, such an attitude would have been unfortunate, but Robert, who was obviously anxious for reconciliation all round, was also the patron of the leading historian of the English, William of Malmesbury, who, as he himself stated, was half-English and half-Norman and anxious not to overpraise or vilify either people. Unlike Geoffrey of Monmouth, Malmesbury was a serious historian and most scrupulous about his facts, but he produced a very individualistic interpretation of the reign of Henry I, by depicting the struggle between Henry and his elder brother Robert as a struggle between England and Normandy. He said that after Henry had married the great-niece of Edward the Confessor, the Normans jeeringly referred to the royal couple as 'Godric and Godgifu',[10] and that Henry, deserted by almost all the Normans, had retained the loyalty of the English, had personally instructed his English troops how to withstand a Norman cavalry charge, and had finally led them to victory over the Normans at Tinchebrai (1106). He concluded that:

It was doubtless by the provident judgement of God that Normandy should be subjected to England on the same day that (forty years before) the Norman army had come to subject her.[11]

No other contemporary chronicler saw the struggle between the two brothers in this light, and William's interpretation remained personal, but the general idea of reconciling Normans and English was undoubtedly 'in the air' and formed the essential background to both William's and Gaimar's work.

The truth of the matter was that it was impossible for the Normans to suppress the English tradition. Just as England was richer than Normandy, so also it had a much longer history which was bound to capture the imagination of anyone with a historical turn of mind. What was more, it was bound to be appreciated for its practical value in establishing the ownership of rights and privileges. The English cathedrals and abbeys, for example, even when they were ruled by Norman bishops and abbots, could only defend their property effectively if they made full use of their Anglo-Saxon charters, and it was often necessary to explain the significance of these by setting them in their historical context. Thus cartularies and histories were often a single work, as at Abingdon, Ely or Ramsey, and recounted not only what the pre-Conquest endowments had been, but also the circumstances in which particular benefactions had been made, how they had been threatened or lost at the Conquest, and how they had (hopefully) been recovered. Details of Norman benefactions were recorded similarly, and the names of the Norman benefactors were included in the convent's commemoratory prayers alongside those of the earlier Anglo-Saxon benefactors.

For laymen the idea of legal continuity was equally strong. At the Conquest each Norman had been given the lands of particular Anglo-Saxons in specified counties, and it was in his own interest to discover precisely what rights his predecessors had enjoyed. It is significant that the word which the Normans used for such predecessors was *antecessores*, because that word eventually became the English 'ancestors', as if the Normans had eventually adopted Anglo-Saxon forefathers. Similarly in the thirteenth century, when the earls of Chester were claiming the (alleged) rights of their *antecessor* in Coventry, they forgot that his real title had been Leofric, Earl of Mercia and called him Leofric, Earl of Chester, just as if he had been one of themselves.

When that stage had been reached, all notion of a real distinction between Norman and English had vanished, because the Normans had projected themselves into the past and identified themselves with the pre-Norman history of England. Both imaginatively and materially that history was very much richer than the pre-Norman history of Normandy and it already had a copious literature. The Normans adopted it as the history of the land, and made the land their own by covering it with their palaces and castles, their cathedrals and abbeys, their parish churches and their ancestral tombs, so that every town and village took on a new appearance and proclaimed their lordship. They belonged to England as much as England belonged to them.

By the end of the twelfth century the Normans in England were ceasing to call themselves Normans. Though modern historians obstinately refer to the exploits of the 'Normans' in Ireland in the 1170s and 1180s, no one at the time described them as that. Most often they were recognized as individual adventurers – Gerald of Wales thought of them primarily as members of his own family – but if they had to be described by a collective or national name, it was not 'Norman' but 'English'. The change was universal because from 1154 even the King of England was not a Norman. Henry II was an Angevin of the Plantagenet family, and only one of his eight great-grandparents had been a Norman; he was buried, as was

131

fitting, neither in Normandy nor in England, but at Fontevrault in Anjou.

King John's loss of Normandy in 1204 merely put the seal on a development which was already virtually complete. The French conquest of Normandy proved to be almost as easy as had been the Norman conquest of England, and those lords who still had lands on both sides of the Channel had to choose, not between England and Normandy, but between England and France. Those who opted for France became French almost without a murmur. In spite of all the difficulties of the transfer, there was never anything resembling a Norman 'national' revolt. The Norman frontiers were not, and never had been, an 'iron curtain', and there were probably as many Frenchmen and Normans with lands on both sides of the land frontier as there were Anglo-Normans with lands on both sides of the Channel. The French continued to refer to Normandy, recognized it as an exceptional province, and observed its Norman customs or laws, but all the evidence suggests that in any real sense of the word there were no Normans left. The kings of England and France had forced the barons of Normandy to choose between their two countries, and no one stood up to protest that he was neither English nor French, but Norman. On the contrary the English became more English and the French more French, and the Normans, as history had known them, disappeared.

69 St Michael and the Dragon, from the Jumièges Gospels. Eleventh-century Norman work showing much English influence (cf. Pls. 26, 27).

Notes

Abbreviations

Alexiad: The Alexiad of Anna Comnena, trans. E. R. A. Sewter (Harmondsworth, 1969).

Amatus: Storia dei Normanni di Amato di Montecassino, ed. V. de Bartholomeis (Fonti per la Storia d'Italia, Roma, 1935).

A.N.: Annales de Normandie.

Apulia: Guillaume de Pouille: La Geste de Robert Guiscard, ed. M. Mathieu (Palermo, 1961).

Benoît: Chronique des ducs de Normandie, par Benoît, ed. C. Fahlin, 3 vols. (Uppsala, 1951–67).

Bourgueuil: Les Oeuvres Poétiques de Baudri de Bourgueuil, ed. Phyllis Abrahams (Paris, 1926).

B.S.A.N.: Bulletin de la Société des Antiquaires de Normandie.

Carmen: The Carmen de Hastingae Proelio of Guy Bishop of Amiens, ed. and trans. C. Morton and H. Muntz (Oxford Medieval Texts, Oxford, 1972).

Dudo: Dudo de St Quentin: de Moribus et Actis primorum Normanniae Ducum, ed. J. Lair (Société des Antiquaires de Normandie, 1865) (cf. P.L. 141).

Fauroux: M. Fauroux, Recueil des Actes des Ducs de Normandie, *911–1066* (Mems. de la Soc. des Antiquaires de Normandie, XXXVI, 1961).

Gaimar: L'Estoire des Engleis by Geffrei Gaimar, ed. Alexander Bell (Anglo-Norman Text Soc., 1960). For translation, see the edition by T. D. Hardy and C. T. Martin, 2 vols. (R.S.) (London, 1888–9).

Huntingdon: Henrici Archidiaconi Huntendunensis, Historia Anglorum, ed. T. Arnold (R.S.) (London, 1879).

Jumièges: Guillaume de Jumièges, Gesta Normannorum Ducum, ed. J. Marx (Soc. de l'Hist. de Normandie, Rouen and Paris, 1914).

Malaterra: Gaufredus Malaterra: de Rebus Gestis Rogerii Calabriae et Siciliae Comitis et Roberti Guiscardi ducis fratris eius ed. E. Pontieri (Rerum Italicarum Scriptores, Vol. I, Bologna, 1928).

Malmesbury: Willelmi Malmesbiriensis Monachi, De Gestis Regum Anglorum, ed. W. Stubbs, 2 vols. (R.S.) (London, 1887–9).

Monmouth: Geoffrey of Monmouth: the History of the Kings of Britain, trans. L. Thorpe (Harmondsworth, 1966).

Orderic: The Ecclesiastical History of Orderic Vitalis, ed. and trans. M. Chibnall (Oxford Medieval Texts, Vols. II–IV, Oxford, 1969–73).

P.L.: Patrologia Latina Cursus Completus, ed. J. P. Migne.

134

Poitiers: *Guillaume de Poitiers: Histoire de Guillaume le Conquérant,* ed. and trans. R. Foreville (Classiques de l'Histoire de France au Moyen Age, Paris, 1952).

R.S.: Rolls Series.

Torigni: Chronicle of Robert de Torigni, in *Chronicles of the Reigns of Stephen, Henry II and Richard I,* ed. R. Howlett, IV (R.S.) (London, 1889).

T.R.H.S.: *Transactions of the Royal Historical Society.*

Wace: *Le Roman de Rou de Wace,* ed. A.J. Holden, 2 vols. (Soc. des Anciens Textes de France, Paris, 1970).

Introduction

1 Cf. the cautious note sounded by G. W. S. Barrow in 'Les familles "normandes" d'Ecosse', in *A.N.,* 15 (1965), 493–515.

2 D.C. Douglas, *The Norman Achievement* (London, 1969), 215.

3 C.H. Haskins, *The Normans in European History* (Boston and New York, 1915; repr. of 1959), 247.

4 Evelyn Jamison, 'The Sicilian Monarchy in the Mind of Anglo-Norman Contemporaries', in *Proc. Brit. Academy,* xxiv (1938), 243.

5 *Orderic* iv, p. xiii.

6 Douglas, op. cit., 218.

1 Normandy and the Northmen

1 *Dudo,* 167.

2 *North-West France,* ed. Findlay Muirhead and Marcel Monmarché (The Blue Guides, 2nd ed., 1932), p. xx.

3 See esp. J. Adigard des Gautries, *Les noms de personnes scandinaves en Normandie de 911 à 1066* (Lund, 1954) and his articles in *A.N.,* 1951–5.

4 F. M. Stenton, 'The Scandinavian Colonies in England and Normandy', in *T.R.H.S.,* 4th series, xxvii (1945), 1–12; reprinted in *Preparatory to Anglo-Saxon England,* ed. D.M. Stenton (Oxford, 1970), 335–45.

5 *Jumièges,* 74–8.

6 Lucien Musset, 'Les domaines de l'époque franque et les destinées de la régime domaniale', in *B.S.A.N.,* xlix (1942–5), 7–97.

7 For what follows, see J. Yver, 'Contribution à l'étude du développement de la compétence ducale en Normandie', in *A.N.,* vii (1958), 139–83; 'Les premières institutions du duché de Normandie', in *Settimane di Studio,* xvi (Spoleto, 1969), 299–366; J. Dhont, *Etudes sur la naissance des principautés territoriales en France (IXe–Xe siècles)* (Bruges, 1948); and J.F. Lemarignier, *Recherches sur l'hommage en marche et les frontières féodales* (Lille, 1945).

8 *Alexiad,* 328.

9 *Apulia* ii, 154–6.

10 D. C. Douglas, *William the Conqueror* (London, 1964), 86; cf. Douglas, 'The Rise of Nor-

mandy', in *Proc. British Academy*, xxxiii (1947), 101–31.

11 For the Church, see Douglas, *William the Conqueror* and 'Les Évêques en Normandie, 1035–1066', in *A.N.*, viii (1958), 87–102.

12 For the monasteries, see Lucien Musset, 'Les destins de la propriété monastique durant les invasions normandes (IXᵉ–XIᵉ siècle) et l'exemple de Jumièges' in *Jumièges* (Rouen, 1955), 49–55; and his 'La contribution de Fécamp a la reconquête monastique de la basse Normandie (990–1066)' in *L'Abbaye Bénédictine de Fécamp* (Fécamp, 1959), i, 57–66.

13 *Orderic* ii, 11.

2 The Norman myth

1 In his edition, Jules Lair attempts to justify the most unlikely of Dudo's statements. For a more critical view see H. Prentout, *Etude critique sur Dudon de Saint-Quentin* (Paris, 1916). Sir Henry Howarth's 'A criticism of the Life of Rollo as told by Dudo of Saint-Quentin', in *Archaeologia*, xlv (1877–80), 235–50 still has value.

2 Dudo was still only a canon of Saint-Quentin in 1015 (*Fauroux*, No. 18, cf. No. 13).

3 *Dudo*, 146–7. Cf. the monk of Caen's story of the smith of Beauvais (p. 69).

4 E.g. in the *Carmen*, Bayeux Tapestry, *Poitiers* and the monk

of Caen. Baudri de Bourgueuil's *Carmen cxcvi* (c. 1099–1102) fits, in this as in most other respects, into the twelfth-century tradition.

5 *Dudo*, 132–4.

6 *Dudo*, 130. The idea of a Trojan origin had been borrowed from the Franks; see J. M. Wallace-Hadrill, *The Fourth Book of the Chronicle of Fredegar* (London, 1960), pp. xi–xii.

7 *Alexiad*, 366–8. Cf. Mathieu's comments in *Apulia*, 46–51.

8 *Dudo*, 154.

9 *Jumièges*, 21.

10 *Dudo*, 169.

11 *Dudo*, 247.

12 *Dudo*, 237.

13 It is so found in two ducal charters of 1009 and 1048 respectively (*Fauroux*, Nos. 12 and 115), and in the fourth book of Hariulf which was written in, or shortly before, 1088 (ed. Bourgin, 162–3, 184–7, 255).

14 *Orderic* ii, 14.

15 *Dudo*, 168.

16 *Dudo*, 181, 196.

17 *Dudo*, 147–8 and 158–60.

18 *Dudo*, 265.

19 *Orderic* ii, 126, referring to William of Echauffour.

20 *Carmen*, line 259, 'Apulus et Calaber, Siculus quibus iacula feruunt'. This comes in a speech by William. Morton and Muntz take it to mean that Normans from Apulia, Calabria and Sicily were present at the battle, but

this seems unlikely. Perhaps the text needs emendation; one would expect the speech to be a catalogue of Norman victories over these other peoples. The line is reminiscent of the inscription on Roger II's sword, 'Apulus et Calaber, Siculus mihi servit et Afer'. However understood, it is difficult to reconcile this line of the *Carmen* with the suggested date of 1067.

21 *Poitiers*, 228. Foreville's note is misleading because of the mistranslation of *propugnant*. See Mathieu in *Apulia*, 339.

22 *Bourgueuil*, lines 305–8.

23 *Malmesbury* ii, 321–3.

24 Ed. R. Howlett, *Chronicles of the Reigns of Stephen, Henry II and Richard I* (Rolls Series, 1886), iii, 186.

3 The Normans of the South: Italy and Sicily

1 *The Travels of Ibn Jubayr*, trans. R. J. C. Broadhurst (London, 1952).

2 Hermann Fillitz, *Schatzkammer*, trans. Geoffrey Holmes. (Kunsthistorisches Museum, Vienna, 1963), 39.

3 *Apulia* ii, 436–8.

4 *Malaterra*, Bk. i, 3.

5 *Apulia* i, 165–8.

6 Douglas, *Norman Achievement*, 3.

7 *Amatus*, 25.

8 *Jumièges*, 187.

9 *Orderic* ii, 98.

10 *Malaterra*, Bk. i, 4–5.

11 *Malaterra*, Bk. i, 38–9.

12 *Malaterra*, Bk. i, 40.

13 M. Yves Nédélec, directeur des services d'archives du département de la Manche, informs me that the earliest certain occurrence of 'Hauteville la Guichard' is soon after 1315: 'Ecclesia de Autevilla, Patronus Guichardus de Monte Forti'. It seems likely therefore that the name of the village derives from this Guichard de Montfort rather than from Robert Guiscard.

14 *Orderic* iv, 68.

4 The conquest of England

1 Most of this paragraph is taken from my article on 'The Norman Conquest' in *History*, li (1966), 279–86.

2 See esp. Brian K. Davison, 'Early earthwork castles: a new model', in *Château Gaillard*, iii, ed. A. J. Taylor (London and Chichester, 1969), and R. Allen Brown, 'The Historian's approach to the origins of the castle in England', in *Archaeological Journal*, 126 (1969), 139–46.

3 *Orderic* ii, 215–19.

4 *Huntingdon*, 231.

5 *Dialogus de Scaccario*, ed. and trans. C. Johnson (London, 1950), 53.

6 For the *Roman de Rou* there is only one MS. of Books i and ii, but four of Book iii. For the *Chronique des Ducs de Normandie* there are two MSS. By con-

trast there are three MSS. of
Gaimar and 186 of Geoffrey of
Monmouth (fifty of them of the
twelfth century).

7 *Gaimar*, lines 4766–79.
8 *Gaimar*, lines 4129–30.
9 *Gaimar*, lines 6447–60.
10 No Norman could debase him-self with an English name, and
though Henry I's wife had been
baptized Eadgyth (Edith) he
had her called Matilda, which
was a respectable Norman
name.

11 *Malmesbury* ii, 475.

Bibliography

I have given references to original
sources and articles in the footnotes,
but now list the most convenient
books for further reading from
different points of view.

General

C.H. Haskins, *The Normans in
European History* (Boston and
New York, 1915).

David C. Douglas, *The Norman
Achievement* (London, 1969).

Normandy

David C. Douglas, *The Rise of
Normandy* (London, 1947; repr.
from *Proc. Brit. Academy*, xxxiii).

William the Conqueror (London,
1964).

Michel de Boüard (ed.), *Histoire de
la Normandie* (Toulouse, 1970).

Lucien Musset, *Les Invasions: le
second assaut contre l'Europe chré-
tienne* (*vii*e–*xi*e *siècles*) (Paris,
1965).

*Normandie romane: i, Basse Nor-
mandie; ii, Haute Normandie* (La
Pierre-Qui-Vire, 1967, 1974).

England

H.R. Loyn, *The Norman Conquest*
(London, 1965).

R. Allen Brown, *The Normans and
the Norman Conquest* (London,
1969).

Sir Frank Stenton (ed.), *The Bayeux
Tapestry* (London, 1957).

Sir Alfred Clapham, *English
Romanesque Architecture: ii, After
the Conquest* (Oxford, 1934).

Italy and Sicily

John Julius Norwich, *The Normans
in the South, 1016–1130* (London,
1967).

*The Kingdom in the Sun, 1130–
1194* (London, 1970).

Evelyn Jamison, *The Sicilian
Monarchy in the Mind of Anglo-
Norman Contemporaries* (London,
1938; repr. from *Proc. Brit.
Acad.*, xxiv).

The Admiral Eugenius of Sicily
(London, 1957).

E. Bertaux, *L'Art dans l'Italie
méridionale: de la fin de l'empire
romain a la conquête de Charles
d'Anjou* (Paris, 1904).

Otto Demus, *The Mosaics of
Norman Sicily* (London, 1950).

List of Illustrations

24 West front, abbey church of Notre Dame, Jumièges, 1037–66. Photo James Austin.

25 Twelfth-century illuminated initial. MS. lat. 2342 fol. 163, *Bibliothèque Nationale, Paris.*

26 Canon tables. From Gospel Book from Jumièges, 11th century. Add. MS. 17739 fol. 5, British Library. Photo Courtauld Institute of Art, University of London.

27 St Matthew. From Gospel Book from Jumièges, 11th century. Add. MS. 17739 fol. 69, British Library. Photo Courtauld Institute of Art, University of London.

28 First page of Dudo of St Quentin, *De moribus et actis primorum Normanniae ducum,* written at the abbey of Jumièges, 12th century. MS. Y. 11. fol. 1 (1173), *Bibliothèque Municipale, Rouen.*

29 Marriage of Duke Rollo to the daughter of Charles the Simple, King of France. From *Chroniques de Normandie, c.* 1475. Yates Thompson MS. 33 fol. 24v, *British Library.*

30 Duke Richard the Fearless superintends the rebuilding of the church at the abbey of Fécamp. From *Chroniques de Normandie, c.* 1475. Yates Thompson MS. 33 fol. 74, *British Library.*

31 The murder of Duke William Longsword. From *Chroniques de Normandie, c.* 1475. Yates Thompson MS. 33 fol. 35v, *British Library.*

32 Duke Rollo landing at Jumièges and his reception at the Porte St Martin. From *Chroniques de Nor-*

mandie, c. 1475. Yates Thompson MS. 33 fol. 1, *British Library.*

33 Dragon sculpture in spandrel of one of the nave arcades, Bayeux Cathedral, *c.* 1150. Photo Courtauld Institute of Art, University of London.

34 Nave interior looking east, Monreale Cathedral, Sicily, 12th century. Photo A. F. Kersting.

35 Mosaic of Christ crowning King Roger II, Martorana, Palermo, 1143–51. Photo Scala.

36 Coronation mantle of Roger II of Sicily, from Palermo imperial workshop, 1133–4. Kunsthistorisches Museum, Vienna. Photo Meyer.

37 Allegorical mosaic, King's private chamber, Palermo, 12th century. Photo Scala.

39 Bird mosaic, King's private chamber, Palermo, 12th century. Photo Scala.

40 Mosaic of the Admiral George of Antioch prostrate before the Virgin, Martorana, Palermo, 1143–51. Photo Scala.

41 Mosaic of William II offering Monreale Cathedral to the Virgin, Monreale Cathedral, 12th century. Photo Scala.

42 Coin minted under Roger II of Sicily. By courtesy of the Trustees of the British Museum.

43 Coin minted under Roger II of Sicily. By courtesy of the Trustees of the British Museum.

44 Death of William the Good attended by a doctor and an astrologer, with the people of Palermo

sorrowing below. Manuscript of Peter of Eboli, Codex 120 fol. 27, *Bürgerbibliothek, Bern.*

46 Archivolt sculpture of soldiers on north door of St Nicholas, Bari, late 11th century. Photo Courtauld Institute of Art, University of London.

47 West front, St Nicholas, Bari, late 11th century. Photo James Austin.

48 Ambulatory interior, Aversa Cathedral, *c.* 1150. Photo Courtauld Institute of Art, University of London.

49 Tomb of Bohemond, Canosa, 1111–18. Photo Courtauld Institute of Art, University of London.

50 Royal tomb, Palermo Cathedral. Photo A. F. Kersting.

51 Columns in cloister, Monreale Cathedral. Photo Bernard H. Cox.

52 William of Jumièges presenting his book to King William. From William of Jumièges, *Gesta Normannorum*, 12th century. MS. Y. 14 (1174) fol. 116, *Bibliothèque Municipale, Rouen.*

53 Silver penny with head of William I. Design attributed to Theodoric, 1068. *National Portrait Gallery.*

54 Writ of William I granting an exchange between Urse d'Abetot and Robert de Lacy. Duchy of Lancaster, Royal Charter. Photo Public Record Office, London.

55 Conan offers the keys of Dinant to William. Detail from the Bayeux Tapestry, 11th century. Episcopal Museum, Bayeux. Photo Archives Photographiques.

56 Constructing the wooden fortress and its earthworks at Hastings. Detail from the Bayeux Tapestry, 11th century. Episcopal Museum, Bayeux. Photo Giraudon.

57 Clifford's Tower, York, 13th century. Photo John Bethell.

58 Rochester Castle keep, built soon after 1126. Photo Crown copyright, reproduced with permission of the Controller of HM Stationery Office.

59 Oxford Castle, built *c.* 1074. Photo A. F. Kersting.

60 Crossing tower, St Albans Abbey, 1077–88 continuing to 1115. Photo Courtauld Institute of Art, University of London.

61 View east along south nave aisle, Norwich Cathedral, *c.* 1120. Photo John Bethell.

62 Lion's head doorknocker, Durham Cathedral. Photo John Bethell.

63 Castle Acre Priory, Norfolk, 12th century. Photo Edwin Smith.

64 View of Durham Cathedral, 1093–1133. Photo Edwin Smith.

65 Nave interior looking east, Gloucester Cathedral, begun 1087. Photo Sidney Pitcher.

66 Westminster Hall, London. Photo A. F. Kersting.

67 Page from the Domesday Book. Photo Public Record Office.

68 Excerpt from Gaimar's *L'Estoire des Engleis.* Durham Cathedral library MS. C. IV. 27 ff. 96v–97r. The Dean and Chapter of Durham.

69 The Archangel Michael vanquishing the devil. From Gospel Book from Jumièges, 11th century. Add. MS. 17739 fol. 19, *British Library.*

141

Index

144